FORSYTH COUNTY
HISTORY STORIES

The Cumming Bandstand, built in 1915, is the oldest structure on the town square. Frank Halstead examines a recent paint job by his crew to aid in preserving the bandstand.

THE
MAKING OF AMERICA
SERIES

FORSYTH COUNTY
HISTORY STORIES

ANNETTE BRAMBLETT
HISTORICAL SOCIETY OF FORSYTH COUNTY

ARCADIA
PUBLISHING

Published by Arcadia Publishing,
Charleston SC, Chicago IL, Portsmouth NH, San Francisco CA

Printed in the United States of America

Library of Congress control number: 2002106704

For all general information contact Arcadia Publishing at:
Telephone 843-853-2070
Fax 843-853-0044
E-Mail sales@arcadiapublishing.com
For customer service and orders:
Toll-Free 1-888-313-2665

Visit us on the Internet at www.arcadiapublishing.com

Front cover: *This photograph is of a crowd at the Fescue Festival, eating a lunch of fried chicken on the courthouse grounds. The white building in the background is Mary Alice Hospital.*

CONTENTS

ACKNOWLEDGMENTS

The preparation of this work would have been impossible without the support and contributions of numerous individuals in varied capacities. First, I would like to thank my husband Rupert Bramblett for his patience, suggestions, proofreading, and willingness to share his knowledge from having lived in Forsyth County for 83 years and witnessing first-hand decades of its history.

To members of the historical society—especially the officers—I appreciate your assuming as many of my duties as possible to allow me time to create this volume. And to Frank Halstead, public facilities director of Forsyth County, I am indebted for working the preservation projects into his demanding schedule and for his assistance with documentation of county structures.

Marie Roper, in donating her brother Garland Bagley's collection to the historical society, has furnished a wealth of photos and information. Of a somewhat different nature are the contributions of an original map of schools prepared by Steve Conrad and the sketch of Poole's Mill by Susy Wetz.

Others who have shared family and community treasures include: Owen Jones, professional photographs of the Fowler house and property; Amanda Hamby, photo of the petroglyph; the late Maggie Worley, Matt School album; Clara Mae Cox, her mother's photographs of family, Cuba, and Forsyth County scenes; Patsy Bennett, document from Bennett's Store; George Welch, information on Jot 'em Down; Jean Terrell, Settle and Settle's Bridge photos; Alice Ziegler, Harrell family data; Carol Tribble, documentation on her father's baseball career; Ruth Martin, photo of Dewitt Thomas; Betty Spruill, photo of Cicero Anglin; Sheriff Ted Paxton, data on his grandfather Penn Patterson; and Donna Parrish, her knowledge of local history gleaned from years of research.

The list would not be complete without mentioning Horace and Joan Whitmire, photo and memories of Frogtown School; Ruth Wallace, the school from a teacher's perspective; Linda Ledbetter, outline of her father's career in education; George Benson, Benson photo; Edith Wright, biographical data on her father; Catherine Amos, Mashburn photos; Teresa Bennett and Jean Brannon, photos, genealogy, and other family information; Midge Webb, Farmers and Merchant's Bank photo; Delores Wofford Evans, Wofford photos; the City of Cumming, artist's rendition of the new city hall under construction; Sawnee EMC, photos from the early days of the cooperative.

And last, but not least, my Sawnee School third graders, who enjoyed field trips to historic sites as much as I did—as evidenced by photographs throughout this work.

The Fowler House is a joint preservation project of the Forsyth County government and the Historical Society of Forsyth County. Public Facilities Director Frank Halstead supervises the rehabilitation.

INTRODUCTION

Rich in history, unique in its character, and remembered for its special happenings, Forsyth County has nevertheless followed the heritage and settlement patterns of the rest of North Georgia from the Cherokee Native American legacy to the gold era and, later, moving from agriculture to the period of rapid growth now in progress. What has made Forsyth County an outstanding area?

The answer is the fiber of her people. In the picturesque setting encompassing Sawnee Mountain, Poole's Mill Covered Bridge, rolling farmland, and close-knit communities, leaders such as Hiram Parks Bell, Dr. Ansel Strickland, Hardy Strickland, and numerous others have demonstrated their mettle by standing firm in their beliefs and toiling diligently for the benefit of the populace.

In education, the county has moved from the community field school to the fine institutions in Cumming, to the consolidated schools of later years, and, once again, to community schools.

Medicine, too, has followed the advances of the times, progressing from the country doctor who treated patients in their homes to the more modern hospitals—from Mary Alice Hospital to Forsyth County, later known as Lakeside, and then to the state-of-the-art Baptist Medical Center.

The Civil War was not fought on Forsyth County's soil, but the county furnished her share of soldiers. Cemeteries throughout the county bear testimony to the sacrifices that local families endured as their young men went away to fight for their country—in all major wars.

Out of struggles and hardships has come inspiration. To achieve the almost unattainable has motivated individuals to strive for improvement—in living conditions, such as those brought by scientific farming; in religious elevation, through the growth of local churches; in jobs, often new to the area; and in social conscience, from prejudice to a land of opportunity for all.

Not only have the people been imbued with a sense of determination and an outreach for achievement, but they have been risk takers as well. When cotton prices could not feed the average family, they began growing another crop—chickens. As land became depleted, they planted fescue. Before electricity could reach the rural areas, they purchased Delco systems. When they wanted educational excellence for their children, they upgraded the community schools and sacrificed to send their youngsters to high school.

The mid–twentieth century witnessed an improvement in the standard of living, but thoughts of affluence had still not taken hold. Lake Lanier was bringing an influx of new residents and visitors, but nothing like the hordes that would come after Georgia Highway 400 was constructed in the 1970s and Atlanta "discovered" the beautiful county to the north.

The Brotherhood Marches of 1987 caused residents to reflect on the history of the county, beginning in 1912 with the rapes of two white women and the trial and exodus of African Americans that ensued.

Now, with a population of over 100,000, Forsyth County is not the county it was just decades ago. Nor will it ever be. At present, the area faces some of the most challenging issues it has ever encountered. Looking back . . . efforts are underway to preserve vestiges of the county's history. Looking forward . . . a new era is just beginning.

The two-story chicken house on the Fowler farm may be the only such structure remaining in the county. Frank Halstead is concerned with its preservation.

1. A LAND OF NATIVE AMERICANS

Forsyth County's Cherokee heritage has left a mark on the area—in place names and in the fancies of those interested in history. But were the Cherokee the only Native Americans to inhabit North Georgia prior to white settlement?

Absolutely not. The Woodland Period (1000 B.C. to 800 A.D.) witnessed the settlement of Native Americans along the flood plains of fertile rivers and the beginning of the use of copper, as well as the development of ritualistic and religious systems, including the funeral practice of constructing burial mounds. Subsequently, in about 800 A.D., the Mississippian Period began to emerge. Religious and funeral practices reached their height during this period with the construction of truncated, flat-topped mounds, examples of which may be seen today at Etowah near Cartersville, Ocmulgee near Macon, and Kolomoki near Blakely. Based on an agricultural way of life, the Mississippian villagers planted fields of corn, beans, and pumpkins. With the coming of European traders and the increasing dependency of the Native Americans on these whites and their goods, the Mississippian population declined in the 1500s.

Enter the Creeks. Historian Garland C. Bagley set the period of Creek Native American dominance in North Georgia as the years between 1540 and 1755, and quoted Colonel Benjamin Hawkins's description of this Native American group:

> The Creeks came from the east. They have a tradition among them that there is in the fork of the Red River, west of the Mississippi, two mounds of earth, and here at this place, the Cussetuhs, Conetuhs, and Chicasaws found themselves. They were distressed by wars with red people, and crossed the Mississippi, and directing their course eastwardly, they crossed the falls of Tallapoosa above Tookaubatchee, settled below the falls of Chattohoche [Chattahoochee], and spread out from thence to Ocmulgee, Ocenee, and the Savannah and up the sea coast towards Charleston. Here they first saw white people and from thence they were compelled to retire again to their old settlements.

By the time noted botanist William Bartram traveled through Georgia and conducted his extensive floral studies—traversing North Georgia in 1776—the

The late J.C. Gazaway preserved Native American artifacts from the pre–Native American civilizations to the Cherokee in his museum.

Creeks had lost their land in the northern part of the state and the Cherokees had established their nation to include the area that would later become Forsyth County. (It is important to note here that Cherokees did not own the land on which their improvements existed. All land in the Cherokee Nation was considered tribal.) Bartram became fascinated by the Native Americans, as well as his beloved plants, and wrote the following in his journal:

> The males of the Cherokees are tall, erect, and moderately robust; their limbs well-shaped, so as generally to form a perfect human figure; their features regular, and countenance open, dignified and placid; yet the forehead and brow so formed as to strike you with heroism and bravery; the eye though rather small, yet active and full of fire; the iris always black, and the nose commonly inclined toward the aquiline.
>
> Their countenance and actions exhibit an air of magnanimity, superiority, and independence.
>
> Their complexion of reddish brown or copper color; their hair long, lank, coarse, and black as a raven, and reflecting the like luster at different exposures to the light.
>
> The women of the Cherokees are tall, slender, erect, and of a delicate frame; their features formed with perfect symmetry, their countenance cheerful and friendly, and they move with a becoming grace and dignity.
>
> The Cherokees in their dispositions and manners are grave and steady; dignified and circumspect in their deportment; rather slow and

reserved in conversation; yet frank, cheerful, and humane; tenacious of the liberties and natural rights of man; secret, deliberate, and determined in their councils; honest, just, and liberal, and ready always to sacrifice every pleasure and gratification, even their blood, and life itself, to defend their territory and maintain their rights.

Bartram's description of the Cherokees could not be applied in toto to one of their leaders, however, for when Chief James Vann occupied an area, uncertainty mingled with dread was the emotion of the day.

In the territory that would become Forsyth County, Vann controlled two sections of land improvements miles apart. The Vann Tavern on the Chattahoochee River was operated in conjunction with a ferry connecting what would be Hall and Forsyth Counties. His other holding stood above the banks of the Etowah River in western Forsyth and was the setting for the death of this infamous chief. Also known as Blackburn Inn and Buffington's Tavern for the Vann relations who operated the pioneer version of a "hotel," this tavern is still in existence across the road from its original location. In a sad state of neglect and disrepair, the structure sits inside a fence to the right of the Old Federal Road near the present landfill and, doubtless, is mistaken by many as a barn in a cow pasture.

As to the power and influence of Vann, a modern day analogy may be drawn. Were Chief Vann alive today, he would likely be a politician with the power and influence to affect the changes he deemed to his advantage. A natural born leader in his time, Vann, who was only a lesser chief in the Cherokee Nation, nevertheless amassed considerable wealth and manipulated political situations to suit himself.

The Vann Tavern, operated by the Vann family on the Chattahoochee River, was moved to New Echota in 1957 when Lake Lanier was flooded.

Vann's influence was especially felt in the early 1800s when the United States government was negotiating with the Cherokees to construct a road through Cherokee territory to connect the trade centers of Augusta and Nashville. When the final plans were mapped out, Vann had prevailed. The road passed through his improvements, including his ferry and tavern on the Chattahoochee, his structures near the Etowah, and the site of his stately home, built in 1805 at Spring Place, now in Murray County.

Cherokee Chief James Vann was of mixed ancestry, his grandfather James Clement Vann having emigrated from Scotland before 1720 and arriving via South Carolina at Spring Place, where he married half-Cherokee Ruth Gann. Records differ as to the name of the chief's father. By some accounts, he was James Clement Vann, who married Wa Wi Li (later renamed Mary Christiana); others indicate that his father was Joseph Vann. That Chief James Vann had two wives has been clearly documented. Elizabeth Thornton was a mixed-blood, and Margaret or "Peggy" Scott lived in the mansion at Spring Place with their five children, including Vann's favorite "Rich Joe."

It would seem that Vann had a bright future mapped out. Not so. Alcoholism brought out a cruel streak in the Cherokee leader. Cherokee businessman, benefactor to Moravian missionaries, proponent of education for his people—James Vann paradoxically was hated by Native Americans and slaves alike and feared by the white man. He met his fate in February 1809, likely as a result of misdeeds to his wife's family while heavily under the influence of alcohol. Since Vann had murdered his brother-in-law John Fawling in 1807 or 1808, the old Native American blood law of a life for a life may have been invoked. (The husband of James Vann's sister, John Fawling, was also a half-brother of Thomas Buffington, an operator of the tavern.)

A tale of events surrounding the death of Vann in the diary entries of the Moravian missionaries, who were devoted to teaching the Native American children and Christianizing the Cherokee population, was recorded for February 21, 1909 as follows:

> We received the startling news of the murder of Mr. Vann. Here and there he and his had punished Indians for stealing. When one of them refused to surrender, Vann ordered him to be shot. For a few days thereafter, Vann stopped at a tavern of a half-breed, Tom Buffington, about 56 miles from here. While there he drank heavily and became involved in altercations with some of his friends for whom he had taken a violent dislike. He feuded with them, was most abusive, and made violent threats.
>
> Toward midnight Vann stepped out of the tavern and stood out before the open door, when suddenly a shot was fired from without which pierced his heart. He fell lifeless to the floor without the perpetrator being seen. After hearing the shot, Joseph, his son, and a Negro rapidly gathered up the belongings of father and son, including

Vann's "packetbook" with a considerable amount of cash and valuable bank notes. Wrapped in a blanket, Joseph with the Negro fled to his father's plantation on the Chattahoochee River, 13 miles from Buffington's Tavern.

Thus ended the life of one who was feared by many and loved by few in the 41st year of his life. No one knows how deeply this crime depressed us and made us appreciate the forbearance of a merciful God for his children. For Vann had been an instrument in the hand of God for establishing our mission in this nation. Never in his wildest orgies had he attempted to harm us. We could not but commend his soul to God's mercy.

Years later, Eli Sherrill purchased the land near the Etowah, moved the tavern across the Old Federal Road, and erected a stately house on the site. Sherrill's daughter Evelyn Carruth in recent times related a somewhat different version of the story of James Vann and his death as passed down to her by her father:

Vann left the tavern one day with a pot of gold and admonished his people that if anyone followed him, he would kill him or her. Apparently, Vann safely secreted away his gold, yet he could not ensure his own safety. After he had sent word to a certain individual that if he ever saw him he would kill him, the targeted man arranged for another person to enter the tavern where Vann was drinking and playing cards. The latter person left the door slightly ajar to enable the threatened man to shoot the chief through the narrow opening in the inn's doorway.

Vann's body was purportedly buried approximately one-quarter-mile away near the Old Federal Road in a graveyard which would later be called the Lewis Blackburn Cemetery. On a board across Vann's grave, the following epitaph was written:

> *HERE LIES THE BODY OF JAMES VANN*
> *HE KILLED MANY A WHITE MAN*
> *AT LAST BY A RIFLE BALL HE FELL*
> *AND THE DEVILS DRAGGED HIM OFF TO HELL*

Fearing for his life and concerned with the disposition of his property, James Vann had written a will in Jackson County on May 8, 1808 to bequeath his household furniture to his wife Peggy and the remainder of his estate to his son Joseph. His plans, however, were negated by the Inferior Court of Jackson County by deferring to the ruling of a Cherokee council, which distributed the estate to include each of his children.

Later, in conjunction with the Gold Lottery of 1832, the Cherokees were dispossessed of their improvements on what had once been tribal land and the two taverns eventually passed into the hands of white settlers.

The Vann Tavern, located on the Chattahoochee, later became the home of Frank Boyd. The Blackburn Inn near the Etowah became the focus for yet another captivating story; in 1819, President James Monroe, fifth president of the United States, is believed to have slept there. Traveling through Cherokee territory, later to be Forsyth County, the President is thought to have spent one or two nights at Blackburn Inn, the setting for Vann's murder.

Monroe spent the night of May 22 in Athens, Georgia and reached Jefferson for lunch on May 23. Then crossing into the land of the Cherokees at Vann's Ferry on the Chatttahoochee, the President may have stayed at Blackburn Inn only the night of May 23; or he may have also remained at the inn on May 24. At any rate, he arrived at Spring Place—near modern day Chatsworth—on May 25.

While President Monroe was at Blackburn Inn, Methodist minister William Jasper Cotter documented his visit in his autobiography: "He was traveling by stage coach and was followed by another coach with his luggage. After supper that night, a bunch of cattle drovers were sitting around and one of them said, 'I wish that drummer salesman would open up his trunks and cases; there might be something that we would like to buy.' " However, because Monroe was traveling incognito through the Cherokee Nation, the inn keeper Lewis Blackburn refrained from revealing the President's identity.

Ownership of the land in the Cherokee Nation was to change drastically in the years to come. The holdings of the Vann family in North Georgia were

This tavern, built about 1804 near the Etowah River, was owned and managed by relatives of the Vanns. At different times, it was known as Buffington's Tavern and Blackburn Inn.

15

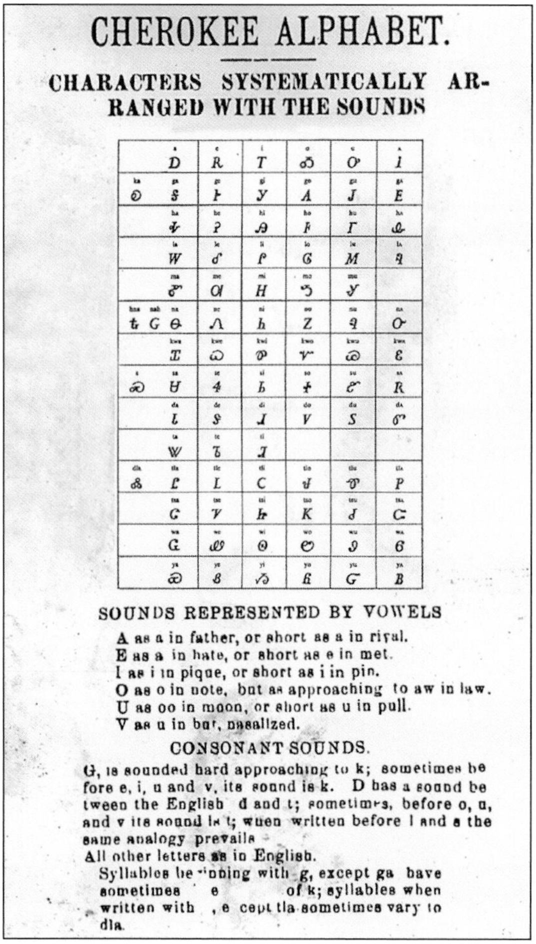

CHEROKEE ALPHABET.

CHARACTERS SYSTEMATICALLY ARRANGED WITH THE SOUNDS

D	R	T	ᴆ	Oʻ	i
Ꮄ	Ꮪ	Ꮅ	y	Ꭺ	Ꭻ	E
Ꮙ	Ꮗ	Ꮎ	Ꮧ	Γ	Ꮒ
W	ꭰ	Ꮈ	Ꮆ	M	Ꮕ
ꮧ	Ꭷ	H	Ꮳ	Ꮿ
Ꮏ Ꮐ Ꮕ	Ꭿ	Ꮞ	Z	Ꮙ	Ꮼ
Ꮓ	Ꮜ	Ꮗ	�	Ꮜ	Ꮛ
Ꮲ	Ꮒ	4	Ꮦ	Ꮩ	R
Ꮮ	Ꮥ	Ꮰ	V	S	Ꮚ
W	Ꮬ	Ꮰ			
Ꮷ	Ꮮ	L	C	Ꮳ	Ꮴ	P
Ꮐ	Ꮙ	Ꮒ	K	Ꮧ	Ꮳ
Ꮐ	Ꮤ	Ꮹ	Ꮎ	Ꮒ	Ꮾ
Ꮷ	Ꮳ	Ꮯ	Ꮂ	Ꮳ	B

SOUNDS REPRESENTED BY VOWELS

A as a in father, or short as a in rival.
E as a in hate, or short as e in met.
I as i in pique, or short as i in pin.
O as o in note, but as approaching to aw in law.
U as oo in moon, or short as u in pull.
V as u in but, nasalized.

CONSONANT SOUNDS.

G, is sounded hard approaching to k; sometimes be fore e, i, u and v, its sound is k. D has a sound be tween the English d and t; sometimes, before o, u, and v its sound is t; wuen written before l and s the same analogy prevails
All other letters as in English.
Syllables beginning with g, except ga have sometimes   e   of k; syllables when written with   , e cept tla sometimes vary to dla.

Sequoyah invented a syllabary, which enabled the Cherokees to have a written language. A few years later, Moravian mission schools were set up to teach the Cherokee to read.

relinquished and the Vann Tavern passed to white landholders. As previously noted, the former Vann property along the Chattahoochee was sold to the Boyd family near the mid–nineteenth century. The fate of the Vann Tavern on this site may not present as sensational a story as that of a presidential visit; nevertheless, it is a historical progression into the twentieth century worth recounting.

William Boyd, a Forsyth Countian who sought his fortune in the California Gold Rush, was able to amass enough gold to return to Forsyth County and purchase the old James Vann tavern, ferry, and several hundred acres of land on the Chattahoochee River near the northeast Forsyth County community known as Oscarville. Recently discovered—misfiled in the historical society's Garland Bagley Collection—was a scrap of paper that the historian had saved in reference to the structure known to many as the Vann Tavern and the land on which it stood:

> William Boyd . . . bought the place from a Mr. McAfee in 1852 or
> around that time. The ferry crossed the river . . . at the upper end of

the bottoms on the Boyd place. On the other side a Mr. Winn owned the place at that time. Later the ferry was moved up the river about 40 yards and went by the name of Williams Ferry—and went by that name as long as a ferry was there.

The Vann Tavern on the land purchased by William Boyd in the 1850s was converted to a dwelling house for members of the Boyd family. In fact, with siding and white paint, the structure closely resembled other homes in the area. Although the house remained in the Boyd family's possession for decades, the flooding of Lake Lanier brought about a drastic change. Frank Boyd, grandson of William Boyd, was faced with the rising waters of the lake as it filled in the mid–1950s. The Georgia Historical Commission came to the rescue, instrumental in supervising the house being taken apart, log by log, and reassembled—sans weatherboarding—at the former Cherokee capital of New Echota near Calhoun, Georgia. And reassembled it was, though not as a dwelling house. The tavern owned by the Cherokee chief is preserved today as it was in the days when weary travelers entering or departing from the Cherokee Nation could stop for entertainment and lodging. Individuals drawn to Cherokee history need only take a day's trip to visit the historic site in Gordon County and to view first–hand the tavern of the powerful chief.

Vann structures aside, the saga of the Cherokees, their progress in the ways of the white man and their struggles to keep their homeland, must be related as an integral part of the historical background of Forsyth County and North Georgia. For decades, the Cherokees of North Georgia and the Forsyth County area attempted to adopt and adapt to the ways of the Caucasians that entered their territory and, for as long, their efforts were thwarted by the greed and animosity of those they sought to emulate.

In endeavoring to adapt to the white man's culture—in trade, money, agriculture, government, shelter, and religion—the Cherokees were limited in their development by the absence of a written language. By 1820, they seriously needed a system for recording and preserving treaties and events, as well as carrying on business and trade. How were the Cherokees to educate their people without the written word?

Onto the scene strode an outstanding half-breed named Sequoyah, who accepted the challenge of creating a written language for his people. Sequoyah had become obsessed by an idea, which had seized him in about 1809, that the syllables of the Cherokee language could be set down in writing on what he referred to as "talking leaves." Years later, scorned and mistrusted by the Cherokees in his own village, Sequoyah completed his syllabary of the Cherokee language only to have his humiliated wife toss the bark on which his creation was recorded into the fire. Patient and methodical, Sequoyah again labored to produce a syllabary for his people. Having attached symbols to 86 syllables, he convinced his influential friend George Lowery to give his invention a test. The test was successful and Sequoyah ascended from the status of a "witch" to that of a hero. Within a few months, several thousand Cherokees had become proficient in reading and writing the language and the culture of these Native Americans was being preserved.

Lest the reader wonder of other significant achievements of the Cherokees, he or she has only to visit the site of New Echota, the capital of the Cherokee Nation, established in 1825. (The site is located in the present day Gordon County.) The skeptic may walk the streets of the once-thriving Native American town and visit the print shop where the *Cherokee Phoenix* was published, the replica of the courthouse that dispensed Native American justice, the restored Vann Tavern moved from Forsyth County, or the home of the missionary Reverend Samuel Worcester who strove diligently to educate and Christianize the Cherokee people. After visiting the capital of the Cherokees, one should ask, "Were it not for the white man's greed, what would have been the progress of the Cherokees and what would the Forsyth County area have become?" Rhetorical questions, yes, but the question of the treatment of the Cherokees and their ultimate removal remains a dark blot in the annals of white expansionism.

To say that the Cherokees continued to live freely according to their tribal customs in North Georgia even after their establishment of a capital and justice system fashioned after the white man's laws would be a misstatement, for the white man's desire for land and greed for gold would precipitate their expulsion to land in the west in less than three-quarters of a century after Bartram's departure from their homeland. Having made treaty after treaty with the white man, the Cherokees experienced emotions ranging from bitterness to despair as these agreements were broken one by one. Beginning with the lottery system, which awarded the lands of the Cherokees to white settlers in 1832, to the offer of lands in Oklahoma, which some of the Native Americans accepted, and progressing to the dispossession of the Native Americans' improvements on tribal land, the end for the Cherokees in North Georgia came with the forced march west in 1838, known as the Trail of Tears.

Lies, deceit, dishonorable execution of agreements, the relationship of the State of Georgia, i.e. the white expansionists, with the Cherokee Indians was fraught with a greed and dishonesty unique in the history of the state from the early beginnings of negotiations to the expulsion of these Native Americans from northwest Georgia.

Yet the end did not come without a valiant struggle on the part of the Cherokees to remain in their homeland. The Treaty of Augusta of May 1783 had reduced the lands of the Cherokees, but this distant tribe was basically left alone for the ensuing 35 or 40 years. However, from 1802 to 1823, the United States government repeatedly attempted to encourage the Cherokee to depart from their homes in the southeast and to accept a reservation beyond the Mississippi. Few Cherokees succumbed to the government's inducements. In fact, the Cherokees of Georgia became even more resolved to hold fast to their homeland.

All the while, white settlers were clamoring for additional land and the government capitulated to their desires by purchasing a large tract in northeast

The late Dorothy Manning sits on seats carved by Native Americans. From the "Indian seats" atop Sawnee Mountain, one has a bird's eye view of the valley below.

Georgia adjoining that ceded by the Cherokees in 1783. Hence, the Cherokee territory was again reduced—this time to an area of northwest Georgia that covered approximately one-sixth of the state. During the years the Cherokees were left more or less in peace, two trends evolved simultaneously: the Cherokees rapidly adapted to and adopted the civilization of the whites, and the intelligent half-breeds gained domination over the Cherokee people. Influential leaders included chiefs such as John Ross, Major Ridge, John Ridge, Elias Boudinot, Charles Vann, George Waters, and John Gunter.

In 1823, President Monroe was rebuffed in his efforts to persuade the Cherokees to migrate west. Adamant in their refusal to leave, the Cherokees fired back at the United States leader with these words:

> It is the fixed and unalterable determination of this nation never again to cede one foot of our land. The Cherokees are not foreigners, but the original inhabitants of America; and they now stand on their own territory, and they will not recognize the sovereignty of any state within the limits of their territory.

Oddly enough, President Monroe upheld the Cherokee claim of absolute ownership and sovereignty, while Georgians protested vociferously.

Subsequently, for two or three years, the Cherokees were left to progress at their own pace. And progress they did. At a constitutional convention at their capital of New Echota, these Native Americans adopted a constitution patterned after that of the United States in July 1827.

Shortly after the framing of this document, the Cherokees and the State of Georgia again found themselves at odds. Like the proverbial irresistible force and immovable object, the opposing sides asserted their determination. On the one side, the Cherokee contended that they were an independent nation with absolute title to their lands. Conversely, the State of Georgia averred that the Cherokee must go—by force if necessary. An act of the Georgia legislature, passed in December 1828 to become effective on June 1, 1830, in effect voided the new Cherokee constitution and nullified the Cherokee government by subjecting the Cherokee Nation to the laws of the State of Georgia. The ulterior motive for the legislation was to encourage the Cherokees to leave the state.

Did Georgia's action accomplish the intended results? If anything, the act of the legislature exacerbated the resistance of the Cherokees. Nonetheless, the Native Americans abandoned their traditional bellicose reaction in favor of fighting the State of Georgia before the Supreme Court of the United States. Grounds for a test case occurred when George Tassel, a half-breed Cherokee, was tried by the Georgia Supreme Court, found guilty of murder in the land of the Cherokees, and sentenced to be hanged. Before the case could be tried in the Supreme Court, however, Governor Gilmer of Georgia not only stated his refusal to appear as a

Numerous gold digging sites dotted Sawnee Mountain. This tunnel was the longest known excavation.

defendant, but ordered George Tassel hanged immediately. Thus ended the first test case, but the Cherokees vowed to try again.

Then the deciding factor, sealing the fate of the Cherokees, flashed into the open in all its yellow glory. Gold! The discovery in 1828 and 1829 sufficed to attract nearly 3,000 adventurers to the land of the Cherokees by 1830—never mind that these interlopers, by their mere presence in the Cherokee Nation, were breaking the laws of the Cherokees, the United States, and the State of Georgia. Having sent numerous proclamations to no avail to the gold seekers to remove themselves from the area, Governor Gilmer escalated his efforts by sending in a company of 75 Georgia soldiers. In two or three months, the lawless individuals were cleared out. To further rid the territory of adventurers, the legislature enacted a law in 1830 that required white persons to obtain a special license before they could reside on Cherokee land. The new law, the legislators hoped, would also rid the area of northern missionaries, who were in open support of the Native Americans.

Meanwhile, the Cherokees had held to the hope of pleading their case before the Supreme Court in an effort to free themselves from the white man's rule. John Ross, leader of the Cherokees, brought suit against the State of Georgia in 1831. Seeking an injunction against the imposition of Georgia laws in the Cherokee Nation, the Cherokees argued on the basis that their land was a "foreign state." The Governor of Georgia again refused to appear as a defendant.

Eloquent speeches and exhaustive arguments having been completed, Chief Justice John Marshall issued the decision of the court in January 1831:

> It has been established to the satisfaction of this court that the Cherokees are an independent and sovereign state, subject to the laws and authority of no other state, nation or power on earth; but they are a sovereign state under peculiar and unique conditions. They are certainly not a state in the United States; neither are they, in the opinion of this court, "a foreign state" within the meaning of the Federal Constitution. Not being a "foreign state," they cannot be competent plaintiffs in this case; hence the injunction asked is denied.

If *The Cherokee Nation* v. *The State of Georgia* proved to be a less than ideal vehicle for pleading the Cherokee cause, the case of *Worcester and Butler* v. *The State of Georgia*, a personal case, would be perfectly suited to the goals of the Cherokees.

With the legislation requiring the licensing of white persons residing within the Cherokee country scheduled to take effect on June 1, 1830, Governor Gilmer became apprehensive when three northern missionaries failed to comply and he gently urged them to obey the law. Reverend Samuel A. Worcester and Reverend Elizur Butler refused. Jailed and condemned to hard labor as a consequence of their deliberate disobedience, the two missionaries captured national attention and became overnight martyrs. The Cherokees at last had the test case they sought.

Worcester and Butler v. *The State of Georgia* was most certainly heard by the United States Supreme Court. For a third time, Governor Gilmer refused to appear as a defendant. And the outcome of the case? Chief Justice Marshall declared the Cherokee Nation independent and sovereign, the Act of the Georgia Legislature extending jurisdiction over the Cherokee country in violation of the United States constitution, and Worcester and Butler, convicted illegally, were to be released at once.

Nevertheless, President Andrew Jackson, an "Indian fighter" in his younger days, refused to execute the judgment of the Supreme Court. With no power to execute it himself, the Chief Justice could only stand by and observe his famous decision virtually negated. Incidentally, Worcester and Butler remained incarcerated at Milledgeville until Governor Lumpkin succeeded Governor Gilmer a year later and set them free.

Adding insult to injury in Georgia's dealings with the Cherokees, the state legislature empowered the governor to have Cherokee lands surveyed and divided into counties in 1831. From one county, Cherokee, ten new Georgia counties were carved out of the lands of the Cherokee Nation. During a brief respite, before more aggression ensued, President Jackson urged the Cherokees to prepare a treaty to cede their eastern territory to the whites. The Cherokees remained unyielding.

In 1832, Georgia dealt the Cherokees another blow. Conducting a lottery at Milledgeville, the state awarded the lands of the Cherokee country to fortunate white drawers. The property having been distributed among the citizens of Georgia, the state legislature enacted a law permitting whites to settle on unoccupied lands, although they were not to intrude on land with Cherokee improvements or to interfere with the Native Americans in any way.

Had President Jackson not supported the State of Georgia in violation of the Constitution of the United States as interpreted by the Supreme Court, this division and distribution of Cherokee lands could not have been accomplished. In complete sympathy with Georgians, Jackson believed it would be in the best interest of all involved for the Cherokees to be removed from the state.

Demoralized and powerless, the Cherokee Nation was divided into two factions regarding the signing of a treaty to cede their remaining eastern lands to the whites. Both the treaty party and the anti-treaty party sent delegations to Washington in February 1835 to confer with the United States government. John Ross, leader of the anti-treaty delegation, presented the terms by which the Cherokees might cede their lands. When government officials deemed Ross's proposal unfeasible, John Ridge of the treaty party presented a plan, which the American government agreed to accept. In a valiant effort to save his homeland, Ross then exerted his influence back home and the Cherokee Nation, required to approve the terms of the agreement for it to become binding, overwhelmingly rejected the proposed treaty. With Cherokee emotions running high, the white settlers in the Cherokee territory feared for their safety, and the Georgia Guard was sent in to protect the whites and friendly Native Americans.

At this point, the State of Georgia threatened to act to resolve the situation by clearing the Cherokees from the state. To avert potential violence, President Jackson decided to invoke the power of the federal government in drafting a treaty with the Native Americans. A convention was called to meet at the Cherokee capital of New Echota (near present-day Calhoun, Georgia). With only the chiefs from the treaty party and a Mr. Schermerhorn representing the United States government in attendance, the business of preparing a treaty proceeded. Drafted and signed only by the chiefs present, the treaty nevertheless was confirmed by the United States Senate and signed by the President two months later over the protestations of John Ross, head chief of the Cherokees.

What were the terms of this treaty that affected the entire band of Cherokees in the eastern United States? Five provisions defined its parameters:

> 1. For surrendering all of their lands east of the Mississippi, the Cherokees were to receive 7,000,000 acres in Indian Territory to which the Cherokees were to remove within two years of the date of the treaty.

William Rogers of Forsyth County was a member of the treaty party when the Treaty of New Echota was signed in 1835.

This petroglyph, which was taken from the Mount Tabor area of Forsyth County, now graces the University of Georgia campus.

2. The Cherokees were to be paid $5,000,000 for their improvements on the ceded land.

3. The United States government would bear all expenses for the Cherokee removal to the Indian Territory; moreover, the Cherokees would receive a year's support after they reached their new home.

4. The Indian Territory was guaranteed never to be annexed to any other state nor would whites be permitted within its territorial limits.

5. The Cherokees were guaranteed the protection of the United States against encroachment by whites and against all foreign and domestic enemies.

The Treaty of New Echota had allowed the Cherokees two years before their required departure. Although over 90 percent of the Cherokee Nation bitterly opposed the terms of the treaty, the position of the State of Georgia was reinforced by the stance of President Andrew Jackson, who believed the only solution to the Cherokee dilemma was their expulsion from the east. Therefore, on May 24, 1838, the date set for the State of Georgia to assume possession of the ceded lands, it became evident that Cherokee resistance would precipitate the use of force in their removal, later to be known as the Trail of Tears.

Subsequent to the signing of the Treaty of New Echota, a census was taken by C.H. Nelson of the Cherokees east of the Mississippi in 1835. The Native

American heads of household in Forsyth County were as follows: Alferd Hutson, George Welch, George Morgan Waters, T.J. Charlton, James Cleland, Martin Brannon, Charles Harris, Sharlot Vickery, Dave Cordery, Samuel Bennett, Sawney (for whom the mountain is named) Bob Tail, Waldeah, William Harris, Henry H. Sutton, Bird Harris, William Rogers, Robert Rogers, Joseph Rogers, Hummingbird, Alfred Scudder, James Kell, Lewis Blackburn, Joshua Buffington, Mose Daniel, Oolskiska, Wickett, and Terrell.

Were all the Cherokees removed from Forsyth County by soldiers wielding the bayonet and herded westward? The answer is no. A few had already migrated. Some who possessed skills of particular value to their communities were allowed to stay, as well as others whose intermarriage among the whites had produced citizens socially acceptable in the newly-converted white man's territory.

Following the Cherokee removal to lands west, a significant artifact was noted in the northwest Forsyth County area near the community known as Frogtown. More than a century later, this petroglyph was transported to the University of Georgia and Forsyth County citizens, wishing to preserve a part of the county's heritage, have been clamoring for its return ever since. Forsyth Countians don't want just a "piece of the rock"—as the commercial goes. They want the entire petroglyph returned to its county of origin. The existence of the boulder was first recorded by George White in his *Statistics of the State of Georgia* in 1849:

> On the road from Cumming to Dahlonega, 10 miles northwest from Cumming, is a very remarkable rock. It is an unhewn mass of granite, eight and a half feet long and two and a half feet wide. It is two-sided, with irregular converging points, upon which are characters, seventeen of them varying in shape. The largest circles are eight inches in diameter.
>
> From its appearance it must have been wrought at a very remote period. The designs are very regular, and it is probable that they were by the same race of people who constructed the mounds in this and other sections of the state. What the characters on this rock mean, the oldest inhabitants cannot tell. The oldest Indians could give no account of it. Would it not be proper for the Legislature to make a small appropriation to convey this curious relic of antiquity to Millegeville?

Milledgeville was at that time the capital of Georgia.

Following a change of ownership of the tract on which the artifact was located, the petroglyph was transported to the University of Georgia for safekeeping. Thus far, efforts to have the rock returned to Forsyth County have been to no avail.

2. FORSYTH COUNTY'S EARLY YEARS

As the historical marker that graces the lawn in front of the courthouse in Cumming attests:

> Forsyth County was created by an act of December 3, 1832 from Cherokee County. It was named for Governor John Forsyth (1780–1841), a native of Frederick County, Virginia, a graduate of Princeton, and gifted Georgia lawyer. He was Attorney-General of Georgia, Congressman, Senator, Minister to Spain, Governor, and Secretary of State under Presidents Jackson and Van Buren.

Incidentally, John Forsyth never set foot in Forsyth County.

The first officers of the county, commissioned on April 20, 1833, were John Blaylock, clerk of superior court; Thomas Burford, county surveyor; and Alston B. Wilborn, coroner. Hubbard Barker was commissioned sheriff on January 31, 1834.

Forsyth County having been officially established, the land was opened to white settlers and fortune seekers. Whether they arrived to establish farms or to mine gold, or both, the migrants to the former Cherokee Nation faced a rugged terrain, Native Americans that resisted departing from their homeland, and lawless individuals bent on easy riches. However, for pioneers who had ventured into the area prematurely—around 1830—an imminent danger lurked in the Wooley's Ford section along what would be the Forsyth–Hall County border at a place on the Chestatee River.

In this untamed land, one faced a plethora of dangers and privations. Among them was outlaw John Murrell, who frequently posed as a preacher when traveling. So great was his charisma that he could enthrall a congregation with his fiery sermons while his gang of thieves relieved the worshippers of their horses and other possessions.

And woe to the person who witnessed this well-rehearsed scheme: he would pay with his life.

The Murrell gang operated out of the Keyhole House at Wooley's Ford prior to the settlement of Forsyth County in 1832.

Just how did John Murrell become firmly entrenched at Wooley's Ford? That question is lost to history, but apparently Murrell, either by establishing a friendly relationship with the Wooley family or through intimidation, commandeered the family dwelling, which would soon be known as the Keyhole House, and perpetrated his violent crimes far and wide from this headquarters.

Until Murrell arrived on the scene, this particular property along the Chestatee had progressed uneventfully through a series of owners. The 246-acre lot was originally drawn by Reuben Powell of Jefferson in the lottery of 1818. Opting not to settle on the land, Powell sold the property to Andrew Taylor. Then in 1830, Margaret Wooley and family gained possession of the acreage and shortly thereafter constructed not only the house, but a mill-dam, grist mill, and sawmill as well.

What attracted John Murrell to the area is unknown and his illegal activities were by no means confined to horse thievery. Murder and mayhem had also followed the "strapping black-haired chap who rode a big bay horse," but his slave-stealing operation was the crime that catapulted John Murrell into infamy. Working along the lines of the Abolitionists, who aided and abetted slaves in their escape to the North, Murrell would encourage slaves to flee to him and would sell these unfortunate people as many as three times with the promise that they would be given a portion of the money that changed hands. When the salability of a particular slave expired, so did the slave. His body was cut open, filled with rocks, and dropped to the bottom of the Chestatee River.

The home of Basil and Margaret Wooley afforded countless opportunities for Murrell's illicit schemes, since its location on the river at Wooley's Ford was at the junction of a rough road and mountain trails. Travelers crossing from the Cherokee country, later Forsyth County, would stop on their way to Gainesville, the nearest destination for traders. Murrell's domination of the house was complete. Over the porch entrance he carved a large keyhole and thereby the name "Keyhole House" was attached to the dwelling. This symbol signified to Murrell's men that friends resided within. In later years, the keyhole came to be associated with the bodies of victims buried in the dark basement and the treasure that was purportedly hidden on the premises.

In addition to the horrors concealed in the bloody basement, the Wooley home featured a room accessible by only a small entrance, where prisoners were supposedly confined. The secret chamber, used to conceal the gang's treasures, could be reached through the ceiling of an upstairs room. In modern times, though, the keyhole over the entrance was boarded over and the hidden room rendered inaccessible except by the removal of a sawed-off rafter.

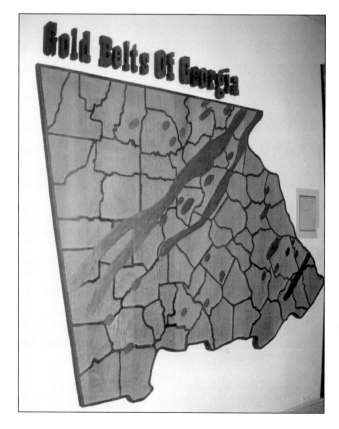

Forsyth County is located in both the Dahlonega and Hall County gold belts. This photo was taken at the Dahlonega Gold Museum.

It is believed that Murrell's forays in North Georgia were of short duration. Having soon married and settled near Jackson, Tennessee, he attempted to establish himself as a "model citizen." At the same time, he and his cohorts were plotting a "wholesale slave insurrection."

During his brief but brutal period in the Wooley's Ford area, Murrell may have used the alias "Guy Rivers." An Etowah River cave, utilized for clandestine meetings by Murrell's gang, was known as the Guy Rivers Cave.

Telescoping the years, the old gray home dubbed the Keyhole House met its fate when Lake Lanier was flooded in the 1950s. The covered bridge and grist mill constructed at the site in 1855 by William R. Bolding had, by popular usage, changed the area's name to Bolding's Bridge.

Less violent, but equally determined, was another group that figured prominently in the settlement of Forsyth County. In the years just before the county was formed, North Georgia was to witness an influx of whites in sizable numbers. What drew these fortune seekers? It took only the whisper that gold had been discovered in the area. It matters little whether they were told that Benjamin Parks found the precious yellow metal in what is now Lumpkin County in 1828, or that John Witherow made the discovery on Duke's Creek in Habersham, now White County, in 1829. The result was the same. The "foreigners" completely overwhelmed the sparsely settled community of Auraria—a word meaning "gold"—in Lumpkin County, the site of the nation's first gold rush.

Forsyth County may never have experienced the frenzied mining activities as did her neighboring communities to the north, but the county was nevertheless located along the two gold belts of the region. The Dahlonega Gold Belt on the northwest and the Hall County Gold Belt on the east ran diagonally through the land that would be carved out of the original Cherokee County and named Forsyth in 1832.

When white settlers were to be allowed into the region by a lottery system, the winning draws were made at Milledgeville for the gold or land lots to be distributed. The lands of the former Cherokee Nation having been surveyed, the 40-acre gold lots in the area that would later become Forsyth County were assigned to fortunate drawers by a method of chance with some winners and some losers.

How much gold did the mines of Forsyth County produce? Certainly the output was nothing to compare to that of Lumpkin County. But neither was the scale of operations. The hydraulic technique, washing away the earth with a powerful water cannon to obtain the gold, was never utilized in Forsyth County as it was in the more mountainous areas.

Placer mining and lode mining provided the means for extracting the precious yellow metal locally. The placer method included obtaining the gold by washing or dredging; hence, the person who worked the streams with a gold pan was known as a placer miner. On the other hand, those individuals who mined the yellow metal from rock beneath the ground were said to engage in lode or shaft mining.

Of the numerous mines scattered throughout the county, the following produced the highest profits according to the gold sold to the United States Mint at Dahlonega: the operations of Harrison Summerour, Hardy Strickland, George Kellogg, Leroy Hammond, Talbot Strickland, Chappley Wellborn, Henry Strickland, and Noah Strong.

A geological report prepared in 1896, *Gold Deposits of Georgia* by Francis P. King, identified the Forsyth County mines as a part of the deposits in the Dahlonega and Hall County Gold Belts and designated the mines by name and lot number.

The Charles Property, owned by Dr. Frederick Charles, consisted of two stringer leads on Lot 77 in the 3rd District and 1st Section. Roughly, this lot is northeast of the Old Federal Road near its junction with Blanton Road and between the Old Federal Road and the Etowah River in the northwestern section of the county.

The Strickland Property, which contained stringer leads, occupied Lots 67 and 68 in the 3rd District, 1st Section. Lot 68 is located on the west side of the Etowah River, while Lot 67 is on the east. Lot 68 adjoins the Charles Property and is northeast of the Old Federal Road near Blanton Road. The Franklin Property was primarily in Cherokee County, but extended across the Etowah River into northwest Forsyth.

The Parks and Fowler Property, with Dr. John Hockenhull as agent and one-third owner, was situated about 9 miles west of Cumming on Lots 933, 934, 935, 936, and 937 in the 3rd District and 1st Section of Forsyth County, and on Lots 973 and 974 in the 3rd District, 2nd Section of Cherokee County.

These lots are north of Canton Highway at the Cherokee County line. Franklin Goldmine Road passes through Lot 934 and Heardsville Road crosses both Lots 937 and 935.

The Sawnee Mountain Property yielded gold only upon the mountain's southeastern slope. Hampton and Herman of Atlanta, having obtained control of Lots 820, 836, 837, 891, 892, 893, 909, 910, 911, 912, 913, 914, 960, 963, and 983 in the 3rd District, 1st Section, discovered that mining with hired manual labor was extremely costly. The two were preparing to convert to a hydraulic system when the titles to the property were questioned and mining operations were suspended.

These lots are situated to the north and south of Bettis-Tribble Gap Road, beginning at a point where the road takes a westward turn—north of Dunn Road. Evidence of prospecting may be seen to the north of Bettis-Tribble Gap Road, where a tunnel and numerous pits still exist.

The Collins Property, located on Lot 450 in the 1st District, 1st Section, was owned by a merchant of Sheltonville, Georgia and worked by Jack Rogers, who dug three shafts and a pit to access the two veins of gold. This lot is north of McGinnis Ferry Road. Boyd Road passes its northeast corner.

The Ad. Campbell Property, named for its original prospector, was situated in Lot 427 in the 1st District, 1st Section. Using slave labor in the 1840s, Campbell sank a 100-foot shaft, ran tunnels in both directions on a vein, and then crushed the gold-bearing ore in a stamp mill on the same property. Lot 427 is located on both sides of McGinnis Ferry Road and abuts the present Johns Creek Technology Park on that development's east boundary.

The Settles Property, in lot 934 in the 2nd District, 1st Section was shaft mined until it was determined that the sulphide vein could not be free milled. Efforts to recover the gold were abandoned. Lot 934 is situated along Settles Road, which passes through the lot in a north–south direction. Grand Cascades Subdivision now extends into the east side of Lot 934.

The Little Property on Lot 420 in the 1st District, 1st Section was owned by Dr. E.D. Little and G.W. Little of Sheltonville. A variety of mining activities occurred on this land, including shaft mining, stamp milling, and placer mining in the branch by Native American lessees. Lot 420 lies to the north and south of McGinnis Ferry Road in both Forsyth and Fulton Counties in the eastern portion of the present Johns Creek Technology Park.

The Favor Property was located on Lots 667 and 668 in the 2nd District, 1st Section about 12 miles northwest of Duluth. Both panning and vein prospecting yielded ore of high quality. The two lots once owned by Favor lie to the north and south of Stony Point Road at its junction with Johnson Road.

Stamp mills like the one in the Dahlonega Gold Museum were used throughout the county to crush gold-bearing ore.

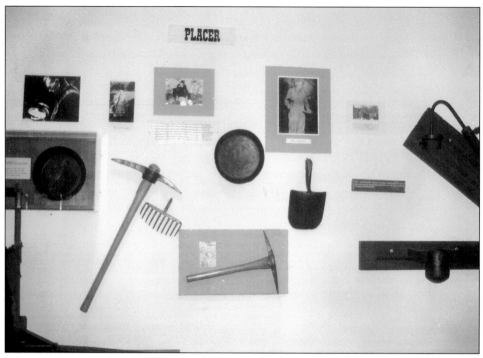

Placer mining tools, like the ones in the display at the Dahlonega Gold Museum, were used in Forsyth County in extracting surface gold.

Other mining enterprises, conducted on a lesser scale than those listed above, included the following:

1. Buice Property, Lot 1081, 2nd District, 1st Section
2. Cowpen Branch Placers on Cowpen Branch
3. Lyons Property, Lot 1259, 3rd District, 1st Section
4. Small stream tributary to Young Deer Creek in southwestern portion of 14th District
5. Mashburn Mine, Lot 70, 2nd District, 1st Section
6. Zamoda Gold Prospect, Lot 1194, 3rd District, 1st Section
7. Montgomery Prospect, five miles southeast of Cumming

In southeastern Forsyth County, the discovery of gold and the concomitant activities relate not only to the mining operations, but to the naming of the community as well. An excerpt from *History of Sheltonville*, prepared by a committee in 1962, follows:

> According to information available, and it could have been quite a long time after this-to-be Sheltonville community was formed, a Mrs. Campbell who with her family lived on top of the hill just beyond and

slightly northwest of where Tom Bell now resides, went to the edge of her yard to empty some ashes. In doing this errand she saw a yellow object gleaming on the ground. She picked the object up, but did not know what it was. Before long someone identified it as a nugget of gold of considerable value. When the news of this nugget being found became known, it created lots of excitement. People who knew about gold and mining came and investigated. It was decided that opening a mine there was justified from the indications of surface evidence. Consequently, several shafts of considerable diameter were dug to depths of numerous feet. Gold bearing ore was extracted from these shafts—in what quantities we do not know. However, a stamp mill was set up on the Cauley Creek about one half mile from the shafts and the ore was hauled there and crushed. Evidently it paid or those old-timers would not have gone to all that trouble.

The gold mining activities shifted from the deep or shaft mining to the surface or placer mining. This type of mining is cheap and easily done, and offers an opportunity to more people to engage in it. There are to this day evidence of extensive placer mining on both Cauley Creek and Cowpen Branch (just north of Sheltonville on the road to Sharon).

In connection with mining in this community is the opportune time to relate the story of how the name of "Shakerag" had its origin. As the story goes, two miners whose fortunes apparently had not been all that could be desired were in the store at what is now Sheltonville one day, and became engaged in a row that progressed to a personal encounter. These two miners' clothing was in a much used and ragged condition. In the action of their fight, their clothes waved and flapped in a grotesque manner. The owner of the store or one of the other respected and substantial citizens of the community separated the belligerents and quelled their row in a rather vigorous manner. As a parting admonition he told them, "Get out of here shaking your rags!" So, the name "Shakerag" came into being.

Moving diagonally across the county to the northeast, to the community known as Ophir along the Etowah River, the story of the Franklin and Pascoe mines and the families associated with the mining industry at that location reads like a best-selling novel—with gold, action, romance, and tragedy. Set on the Cherokee–Forsyth County border, the historic unfolding not only involves a "rags to riches" element, but boasts presidential connections and a hint of politics as well.

The operation known in the latter part of the nineteenth century as the "Franklin Gold Mines" began through the persistent efforts and adaptations of two separate families, the Franklins and Pascoes, and merged into an industry that ultimately involved hundreds of people.

The story began to unfold when Mary Franklin, widow of Dr. Bedney Franklin of Morgan County, per chance drew Land Lot 466 in the newly created Cherokee County in the Gold Lottery of 1832. She immediately began receiving numerous offers from "gold fever"–motivated opportunists to purchase her holdings near the Forsyth County line. Curious as to the interest in her lot lying just south of the confluence of the Etowah River and Settendown Creek, Franklin mounted her mule and trekked the formidable distance alone from Clarke County to investigate first hand the reason others were so eager to acquire her land.

Franklin found that not only did gold exist on her property, but the yellow metal had lured a number of prospectors, who were engaged in removing the ore in determined fashion. Imbued with a sense of self-preservation and bold action, Franklin sought out a trusted friend of her late husband to evict the intruders from her land and to oversee her gold interests while she returned to Clarke County for her family.

The Franklins' initial mining efforts began with the extraction of free gold, i.e. gold not bound with other minerals. Under the supervision of Mary Franklin and her sons, slaves conducted surface mining operations, employing sluice boxes and rockers. The quantity of free gold thus removed from the earth to a depth of 20 or 30 feet netted the Franklins a handsome sum.

Mary Franklin's son-in-law Charles McDonald, Governor of Georgia from 1839 to 1843, owned the lot adjoining the Franklin holdings. Situated along the Etowah River, the Franklin and McDonald veins ran parallel. That the mines were also located on the Alabama Road West and only a few miles from the railroad at Ball Ground rendered them easily accessible to the outside world.

Nothing comes easy for very long and the removal of the free gold from the earth was no exception. Prior to the Civil War, with the supply of free gold depleted, the arduous task of obtaining the gold previously lost in the sulphides necessitated business as well as operational changes. Under the new arrangement, Franklin and McDonald interests were incorporated as the Franklin-McDonald Manufacturing Company, managed by northern capitalists. Colonel A.H. Moore, with capitalization of $250,000, employed "modern" techniques when he constructed a dam across the Etowah, installed a tramway system between the shafts and mills, provided housing for a minimum of 100 employees, and developed a chlorination process for recovering the gold previously lost in the sulphides.

The fairy tale story of the mines and their successful operation could not be sustained indefinitely without tragedy, for, prior to the Civil War, a cave-in of one of the shafts forever buried a number of slave laborers. Tragedy compounded upon tragedy when Mary Franklin's son Bedney was killed in a stamp mill accident. Subsequent to the death of Mary Franklin in 1858, her son Leonidas attempted unsuccessfully to manage the mines. With free milling at an end, the cost of obtaining the gold bound with other minerals outweighed the profits.

The mining era ended for the Franklin family in 1883 when the Franklin holdings—Lots 399, 400, 465, and 466, and portions of Lots 327, 392, 393, 395,

The Pascoe House was built by John Pascoe in the 1840s. His brother Samuel raised a large family in the structure, later a part of the Creighton Mining Company.

398, 463, 541, and 612 in the 3rd District, 2nd Section of Cherokee County—were sold to the Creighton Mining Company. Nevertheless, it has been estimated that the family had realized approximately $50,000 during its continuous years in the mining business.

Land adjoining the Franklin interests involved another family, the Pascoes, beginning with brothers John and Samuel, migrants from Cornwall, England, who arrived at Ophir after unsuccessful mining attempts in the gold fields of Dahlonega. John fared considerably better on property that straddled the Cherokee–Forsyth County border. With a stake from Major Wyley Petty, a prosperous farmer in the area, he leased a 10-acre tract near the Ophir community from the Leonard brothers and erected a five-stamp mill beside the Etowah River. Farming during the growing season—raising cotton and sheep and tending vineyards—and mining during the off-season proved to be a winning strategy, for John Pascoe amassed enough capital to purchase the original 10 acres leased from the Leonards plus the adjoining lots.

In fact, the future appeared so rosy that John Pascoe sent to England for his bride-to-be, who booked passage and embarked for the United States. At his Ophir property, John Pascoe completed a stately home for his intended. The structure was magnificent for its day and location, with a carved mantel imported from England and a separate kitchen that, at first glance, offered the impression of twin structures erected side by side.

Alas, this fairy tale scenario was not to play out as scripted. "Once upon a time" conversely became "once upon a horror" when John Pascoe, working in his mining laboratory one day in 1853, accidentally ingested mercury and, shortly thereafter, succumbed to mercurial poisoning. Pascoe's fiancée, en route at the time of his death, was met with the devastating news of his demise and retraced her steps to England.

Just what did fate intend for the land, mines, and structures thereon? The house so meticulously constructed by John Pascoe would be utilized to the fullest in the century and a half that followed. Upon the death of his brother John, Samuel bought out his siblings' interest in John's estate and, firmly ensconced in the dwelling, raised a large family on the property.

The next segment of the Pascoe saga belongs to Samuel. Born March 4, 1810, Samuel Pascoe married Mary Jackson in Putnam County and thereby allied himself with a southern family of distinction. His wife was the daughter of Joseph Jackson, a brother of General Thomas Jonathan "Stonewall" Jackson, and Elizabeth Booker Jackson.

When Samuel Pascoe died on March 26, 1887 and was buried in Hightower Baptist Church cemetery, he was laid to rest near his youngest child, Mourning Victoria, who died in 1862 while her father was away on a business trip. The family's efforts to preserve the baby's body by laying it in the basement at the foot of the staircase in their home were to no avail. When Samuel returned home, his young daughter had already been interred, another tragic twist in the Pascoe tale.

The Shingle House was a post office and business office for the Franklin Gold Mines. It was located in the center of the gold mining area near the Etowah River.

Approximately two and a half years after the death of her husband Samuel, Mary Jackson Pascoe, born September 7, 1817, passed away on September 15, 1889 at age 82 and was buried in the family plot at Hightower Baptist Church.

Traditions in the Pascoe family portray two of Samuel Pascoe's daughters as spunky young women. As the story goes, one daughter, Catherine, was in the house one day when a suitor whom she detested came to call. Did she meet him in the parlor as the etiquette of the times dictated? Indeed not. By climbing down a holly tree, planted years earlier by her Uncle John, from an upstairs window, she opted to do a disappearing act for the duration of his visit rather than risk betrothal to a man she intensely disliked. Another daughter was at home once when a man called to be put across the river on the ferry operated by the Pascoe family. As all the males of the household were away, Samuel's daughter answered the call and managed the ferry herself. The two immediately fell in love and were soon married.

Departing from the drama of the two families associated with the mines, a look at the mining operations is in order. Prior to Samuel Pascoe's death in 1887, his land had yielded $56,000 in deposits recorded at the United States Branch Mint at Dahlonega. In 1882, the gold properties, about 1,200 acres in toto, were merged under northern capitalists as the Franklin and McDonald Mining and Manufacturing Company. Capitalization of $250,000 enabled resident manager and engineer A.H. Moore to institute the changes, which would maximize productivity. By 1900, a thoroughly modern plant for its day was in operation, complete with new machinery, a dam across the Etowah River, a tramway system between shafts and mills, and several new shafts—one 500 feet, the deepest in Georgia at that time. Historian Roy Bottoms described the mining industry from 1882 to 1910:

> Col. Moore found that the Franklin properties contained almost every kind of gold ore, including free deposits, quartz veins, and gold sulphurites. He helped to invent a new chlorination process for the reduction of the gold from its sulphurites, and also used quicksilver or amalgam process as well as the more modern cyanide process. The employment of these methods at the Franklin Mine marked the only scientific approach on a large scale mining that had ever been in Cherokee County.
>
> In 1883 the vice-president, J.M. Creighton, a wealthy railroad official from Philadelphia, bought out the other stockholders, and the property was thereafter called the Creighton Mine . . . The Creighton Mine, by the year 1886, had an office, assay laboratory, commissary, blacksmith shop, stables, miners' cottages, etc., all substantially constructed and well arranged and this made up the remainder of the Creighton plant. Near the above year, the firm employed some 85 hands, working in two shifts of 12 hours each. The wages received varied from 75 cents to $2.50 a day, according to the class of labor. At the time the entire cost of

mining, milling, and chlorination was around $2.70 per ton. This mine is reported to have had as many as 300 people working for it before closing down in or around the year 1909.

. . . Mr. Creighton died in 1887, and the Manager Moore resigned, and the management fell into several different hands before operations were halted sometime around the year 1909.

In the latter years of mining operations near the turn of the century, the fine, substantial house erected by John Pascoe in the pioneer days of gold mining became the residence of the superintendent of the mines. The superintendent in 1901 was none other than Edward William Axson, the brother of President Woodrow Wilson's first wife Ellen Louise Axson Wilson. Edward William Axson's marriage to Florence Choate Leach having been set for April 9, 1901, the prospective bridegroom endeavored to upgrade the "Pascoe House" to a suitable condition for his bride. Effecting sufficient changes to the dwelling to cause a modern preservationist to shudder, Axson apparently upgraded the structure to the satisfaction of his beloved.

All of the changes Edward Axson made to the Pascoe House are unknown. However, the Axsons were in residence only a few short years when, on April 26, 1905, Axson, his wife, and young son were killed en route to a picnic in an accident at the river. Explosives used at the mines may have been responsible for spooking their team, which bolted and ran, with buggy in tow, onto the ferry and off its far end into the waters of the Etowah, which were deep due to the construction of a dam. Axson, a swimmer, negotiated the river back and forth from wife to child and saved neither. The three perished before nearby miners, responding to an alarm, could hasten to the rescue. The bodies of the small family were transported to Savannah for burial.

More tragedy was yet to come. The vast sums derived from the working of the mines from 1833 to *c.* 1909 suddenly came to an end on the day the Etowah inundated the mines while most of the employees were out at mealtime. So great was the suction from the cave-in that huge oak trees were pulled beneath the water with a fury rivaling that of a severe thunderstorm and thus, the curtain came down on the gold era in eastern Cherokee and western Forsyth County, Georgia.

Before the story is abandoned, however, the account of Dr. George McClure must be related. McClure arrived at the Creighton Mine in 1902 as a young man one year out of medical college to become the company's physician. Paid $25 annually by each family, he made house calls, delivered babies, and dispensed medicine. Around 1909, McClure moved into the Pascoe House, where he resided until his death. The wooden building just across the driveway from his home served for years as his office.

Anyone who believed that the closing of the mines in 1909 would end the fatal accidents on the former mining property was in error. Ironic as the situation may seem, approximately a century after John Pascoe's death from mercurial poisoning, McClure entered his office late one night and mistakenly drank from a jug of medicine—digitalis—intended to be administered in small doses. All attempts to save his life proved futile and he, too, died from ingesting a harmful substance on November 13, 1933.

Moving to the western side of the county, another family, the Harrells, acquired land on the present day Post Road and engaged in farming and gold mining. County deed records indicate that Edward Harrell purchased a 40-acre lot from Edward Kent of Gwinnett County for $100. After Harrell arrived with his wife Nancy Strickland Harrell and children in a covered wagon, he built a two-room log house from the virgin timbers on the land. Surrounding the structure were black walnut and chestnut trees, which yielded a bountiful harvest each fall. A dextrous individual, Harrell began clearing the land, building rail fences from the wood of the chestnut trees, and styling his family's furniture from the black walnut wood. Soon after establishing the family in Forsyth County, Harrell erected an imposing two-story frame house beside the two-room log building and his descendants occupied the dwelling for over a century.

A farmer, yes, but a gold miner, too. Having learned the skills of mining in the Carolinas, Harrell was prepared when Henry Strickland, his wife's brother, discovered gold on what would be known as the John B. Richards farm at Ophir and requested that Harrell help him recover the gold on a share basis (*c.* 1835–1838). So Harrell arrived at the mine with gold pan, picks, shovels, mortars and pestles, and a number of slaves. With Harrell in charge, some of the slaves worked in a pit, while

The late Redger Worley explored the yard of the fine home erected by Edward Harrell in the 1830s. This dwelling house served the Harrell family for almost 140 years.

The late Helen Carroll posed in front of the log barn on the former Harrell plantation. Constructed of hewn logs, the barn was erected in the 1830s.

others sat on the ground and pounded ore with crude mortars and pestles. After several weeks, the gold vein ran out and Harrell requested a settlement. Instead of receiving half the profits as had been agreed upon, he was paid the wages of a hired hand. While Harrell seemed to take the matter lightly, his wife Nancy was angry with the Stricklands for some time to come.

With the advent of the gold rush in California, Edward Harrell and his oldest son Jerry went west to seek their fortunes. Another son Newton came later, but because of poor health, he returned to Forsyth County. He married Mary Ellender Harris and raised a large family of prominent individuals in the house built by his father in the 1830s.

As the gold mining emphasis shifted from North Georgia to California, families such as the Worleys were migrating to Forsyth County to settle on rich farmland. Members of the Worley family in the county today trace their lineage to David Worley, who was born in North Carolina in 1832 and died on December 19, 1890 in Forsyth County. According to family members, David Worley's son Reuben purchased the property later known as the Worley place from a Hill Roberson, who had enlarged the farm's original log cabin. Reuben Worley and his wife Frances Elizabeth Bottoms Worley raised a family of eight in the sturdy structure prior to his death on February 22, 1942. Their youngest son Redger and his descendants would later become the property's owners. The cabin was also home to Cumming City Councilman Rupert Sexton, who spent his early boyhood on the Worley farm.

Following his marriage to Maggie Harrison, Reubin Worley's son Redger eventually returned to the farm where he helped run the syrup mill. His wife described the syrup mill operation by describing how the cane to be ground was fed into a mill, which was powered by a horse that moved a long pole around in a circle; when the juice had been extracted from the cane, it was boiled down to a certain thickness in a copper pan and then poured into jugs. People from throughout the community would haul their syrup cane to the Worley's, for they owned the only mill in the area. Fees for processing the cane for these customers were calculated by the number of gallons of syrup the cane produced.

Redger and Maggie Worley reinforced the concept of "home" by deeding the land to their descendants. And, though they pursued careers, married, and raised families of their own, their four daughters—Louwellen, Nancy, Sue, and Barbara—along with their families, continued to gravitate toward the homeplace. For years, every Sunday at the Worley's resembled a family reunion.

This original cabin with additions was home to Reuben Worley and his descendants. Redger and Maggie Worley and their four children called it home until their new house was erected c. mid-twentieth century.

3. Natural Sites and Public Buildings

From seacoast to magnificent mountains, Georgia is a scenic state extraordinaire and Forsyth County claims her share of the beauty and charm with geographic features and historic structures to provide a link with the past. To begin with a natural site, one could pose the question: what landmark in Forsyth County was the site of gold mines, was named for a Cherokee chief, rises 1,967 feet above sea level, and has been a favorite place for citizens to visit for decades? The answer could be none other than Sawnee Mountain.

Arthur Sosebee, who lived to be a centenarian, reminisced about his interest from the days of his youth in the Cherokee history and lore associated with the mountain. The following is an excerpt from a tape he prepared for this writer in 1975:

> Sawnee Mountain over here was named for an old Indian chief, who once lived in this county. You go out Kelly Mill Road and cross the creek and turn to the left. There was once an old field road that led to an open field, and I have cultivated that field myself. And it is said that this old Indian chief by the name of Sawnee had two living wives, and he built a cabin for each of them. He built a cabin at one end of the field for one wife . . . and at the opposite end of the field he built a cabin for the other wife. I don't know how they got along, but anyway, according to the legend, that's what he did.

Arthur Sosebee then related memories of his visits to the mountain and his impressions of the rock formations north of the Bettis–Tribble Gap area:

> If you look for them, you can see them. It seems that it's eight or ten feet wide with rocks piled together and forming a semi-circle, starting at one point and coming back together at another point at the crest. And nobody seems to know how that mass of rocks came to be there. Perhaps the Indians arranged them as a sort of a wall for protection from some invader. I just don't know, but you look for them, you'll find them.

Sawnee Mountain is Forsyth County's best known landmark. Pictured is the late Ruth Frazer with the mountain in the background in a traditional setting.

Rock formations aside, Cherokee legends abound. A favorite holds that Chief Sawnee, who was considered too old to endure the trek to Oklahoma on the Trail of Tears in 1838, was sealed in a cave on the mountain to live out the remainder of his days. In his poem "Chief Sawnee," the late Forest Wade described the fate of the elderly Cherokee in the final stanza: "On top of Sawnee Mountain where the eagle flew high, Far back in a tunnel Chief Sawnee did die. High up on the mountain, far back in a cave, Lies a great Indian warrior so loved by his braves."

Years after the Native American removal, extensive prospecting was carried out on the slopes of Sawnee Mountain. Pock marks and mining tunnels, which may still be evidenced today, are vestiges from a time when the gold mining industry was a thriving business. The following report by State Geologist W.S. Yeates, entitled *Gold Deposits of Georgia*, was prepared in 1894.

Sawnee Mountain, lying in the heart of Forsyth County, towers in solitary grandeur, 900 feet above the surrounding country, otherwise practically unbroken. Its central summit rises 1,967 feet above sea level; and spurs from this trend from northeast to southwest, making a total length of about six miles. Generation following generation have panned, and in other ways prospected this mass for gold. The metal has been found, however, only upon the southeastern slope.

Geologically considered, the mountain is made up of schists and gneisses, striking northeast, and dipping sharply to the southeast. Interbedded with these, are thick beds of quartzite, boulders of which overlie the surface in such abundance that the mountain is locally considered to be formed entirely by the same. This latter idea, however, may be shown to be erroneous by even a casual examination of the prospectors cuts. One of these, a cut of two hundred feet or more in length, shows a complete walling of schists, with the exception of several quartzite beds, one of which attains the width of 20 feet. Furthermore, a consideration of the laws of natural erosion on different rocks here displayed will satisfactorily explain the presence of the quartzite boulders.

Whether they were interested in mining, Native American lore, or simply enjoying a family outing, citizens have been drawn to the mountain for as long as there have been inhabitants of the area.

From mountain to bridges and streams, the vista in days of yore was equally picturesque. Beginning on the Chestatee River, which forms Forsyth's

Andrew Looper Keith returned from the Civil War and operated a ferry across the Chestatee River between Forsyth and Hall Counties.

This rare photo shows Keith's Bridge, so named for its builder Andrew Looper Keith, who received a government contract to erect the span across the river to connect Forsyth and Hall Counties.

northeastern border with Hall County, Keith's Bridge provided access between the two entities. The span was named for its builder, Andrew Looper Keith, who returned from the Civil War to farm his land and operate a ferry—Keith's Ferry—across the Chestatee. Later, he received a government contract to construct a bridge across the river. The covered bridge erected by Keith and the metal bridge which followed were both dubbed "Keith's Bridge."

Downstream from the Keith's Bridge area and below the confluence of the Chestatee and Chattahoochee Rivers, lies Brown's Bridge, its history delineated by Carolyn Nuckolls Baker:

> In 1816 the Cherokee Indians had been forced west of the Chattahoochee River. By the time Hall County was formed (1822), freight wagons were moving from Jefferson through Gainesville, a trading center, to the west along what is now Brown's Bridge Road. In pioneer days, the only road to the west, the Federal Road, crossed the river at Vann's Ferry, later owned by Richard Winn. The ancient ford, known to white settlers as Goddard's Ford, was shallow, rocky, and unfit for a ferry, and—contrary to some reports—there was never

a ferry at this site. The first Brown's Bridge was probably constructed at this site. A new ferry—also called Goddard's—was constructed just above the old ford site where the water was deeper and more suitable for a ferry. On September 2, 1822, the Inferior Court of Hall County instructed Robert Young and others to "lay out" a road from the town of Goddard's to the Federal Road. Just over the river, this road joined the Federal Road at Hartford, a crossroad that would later be called Oscarville in Forsyth County. However, periodic rises in the river at Goddard's old ford halted traffic for days or longer and was a continuing problem for freight wagons and travelers.

Minor Winn Brown, a Forsyth County resident prior to 1830, a Gainesville merchant, second postmaster of Gainesville, and the owner of property around Goddard's old ford site—on both the Hall County and Forsyth County sides—was authorized to build a toll bridge at the ford site on December 21, 1839 by the legislature. This was the first or one of the first bridges over the river and was built on Minor W. Brown's own property. The tolls he could charge were set by the legislature and are as follows:

4 horse wagon	$0.50
2 horse wagon	0.37 1/2
1 horse or oxen cart	0.25
4 wheel carriage	0.25
Man and horse	0.12 1/2
Loose or led horses	0.06 1/4
Cattle	0.03 each

No known description of this first bridge built by Minor Winn Brown has survived. Through the years several bridges were built to replace the bridge when it was lost in floods or, as said in one case, "blown away" by a tornado. On January 5, 1875, Oliver Clark of Forsyth County bought at auction from the estate of Minor W. Brown one undivided 1/2 interest in Brown's Bridge. The last owner was a Mr. Bester Allen in 1888. In February of 1898, Hall and Forsyth Counties agreed to pay Bester Allen $1,600.00 for Brown's Bridge, thus making it a toll free bridge and improving travel with Gainesville, a major trade center. The last covered bridge was built sometime between 1898 and 1901. It is unclear whether the bridge was rebuilt because it was in poor condition or because it was destroyed by an act of nature. It was a covered bridge and was said to have been erected by a member of the King family of Columbus, Georgia.

The timbers for this last covered bridge were sawed by Truman Lafayette Nuckolls and were taken from his property along Shady Grove Road in Forsyth County. . . . According to Brown family lore,

Mr. Nuckolls also helped with construction of the bridge, and a Mr. A. Claude Benson hauled some of the sawed timber to the bridge site and was the first person to cross this new covered bridge as he hauled the last load of lumber for the bridge. The bridge was held together with wooden pegs. The pegs and the holes were cut the same size; the pegs were then dried to shrink them so that they could be driven into the holes. As the pegs absorbed moisture from the air, they again expanded to make a very tight fit.

Of less significance as a waterway, but fully as rich in history, is a creek known as Settendown. From the days of pre–Native American civilizations, Settendown Creek has witnessed the sheer joy of those taking a dip in its waters, the labor of the millwrights who harnessed its power, the anguish of travelers wishing to cross in times of flooding, the inconvenience of farmers when bridges washed away, the pain of Native Americans who were herded to the West, and the peace and tranquillity of individuals who simply absorb the beauty along its banks.

The upper part of Settendown Creek, formerly called Mill Creek, forms in the northern part of Forsyth County and, as it flows in a generally west-southwesterly direction, it crosses the present-day Settendown Road, Hopewell Road, and Dahlonega Highway (State Route 9). Then, the stream merges with Squattingdown Creek on Land Lot #390 and, thence, with another

Visitors have long enjoyed the rocks below the covered bridge and mill site in the area called Poole's Mill. Glenn Croy, Clara Mae Redd, and C.W. Cox posed for this photo at a favorite spot in Settendown Creek.

The mill depicted in this sketch by Susy Wetz was owned by Cherokee George Welch, then by Native American agent Alfred Scudder, and later by Dr. M.L. Pool. The building was burned by vandals in 1959.

minor creek before it crosses Matt Highway. A short distance southwest of Matt Highway, it enlarges, in part due to dredging efforts, but feeder streams are also a contributing factor. Finally, Settendown, now a full-size stream, flows beneath the bridges of Dr. Bramblett Road, Burnt Bridge Road, Wright Bridge Road, Wallace Tatum Road, and Poole's Mill Road before it recrosses Matt Highway on the way to its confluence with the Etowah River on Land Lot #398 in Cherokee County. Named for Cherokee Chief Sittingdown, the creek has witnessed several pollutions of its name—to the present Settendown. In 1969, the late Forest Wade identified on a map various Native American sites along the creek. From east to west, those locations included Chief Settendown Village, an "Indian mound" on the J.W. Tatum farm, Jacob Scudder's mills, Scudder's home, and one of Chief Rising Fawn's homes.

Local author Eugene Croy's great-grandmother Merveania Kemp Hawkins, wife of John Samuel Hawkins, passed on numerous bits of history and legends before her death on February 10, 1913. One of these stories was the Stage Coach Robbery at Settendown Creek. As the story goes, a stage coach robbery occurred at the site where the Alabama Road forded Settendown Creek. Word had come to the Hightower community that a coach laden with gold was approaching. When the driver arrived at the ford, he purportedly reined in the team to permit the animals to drink from the stream. His mistake. From out of the bushes growing densely along the creek bank, several masked riders bounded from their cover, surrounded the stage, and robbed the driver of several hundred pounds of pure gold.

Speculation was rampant. Were the perpetrators Cherokees or white outlaws? One theory held that the Cherokees were guilty and, after the robbery, secreted the gold in the Hightower Tunnel for safekeeping. Another placed suspicion on a white man who, shortly after the heist, paid for a gun and other miscellaneous items with gold that appeared to have been chiseled from a bar. One question: what became of the remaining gold?

A look at water power provided by Settendown offers a different perspective of the creek. Around 1820, a three-story mill was constructed beside Settendown Creek with slave labor by Cherokee Chief George Welch. The structure's dimensions, according to author Forest Wade, were 45 feet high, 40 feet wide, and 60 feet long. Powered by an overshot waterwheel in the waters of the creek in western Forsyth County, both a gristmill and a sash-type sawmill operated from the same source through the use of pulleys. Chief Welch's days as a miller were cut short by the Cherokee Removal in 1838. All of his property having been appraised at $12,500 by the government, Welch's gristmill alone was valued at $719.50 at the time he was dispossessed.

In the Gold Lottery of 1832, Land Lot 436 in the 3rd District, 1st Section of Forsyth County—the lot on which Welch's Mill stood—was drawn by John Maynard of Jackson County. Shortly thereafter, Jacob Scudder, a brother-in-law of Chief Welch, purchased the lot from Maynard for $250 in 1833.

Scudder owned and operated the mill, then known as Scudder's Mill, from 1833 until near the time of his death in 1870. A deed dated August 8, 1868 conveyed the property from Scudder to his grandsons, Lewis Scudder and William Henry Harrison "Hal" Scudder. In 1880, the mill property was purchased by Dr. M.L. Pool (born 1825, died 1895), the son of Major Benjamin and Matilda Pool and husband of Lucy Caroline Magnum Pool. Hence, the area around the site became known as Poole's Mill and this designation remains to the present.

Bridges served the citizenry in one capacity, as did public buildings—namely courthouses and jails—in another. The story of Forsyth County's courthouses could aptly be titled "From Humble Beginnings," for it is a Lincolnesque tale complete with log cabin origin. The town of Cumming was laid out in 1834 on Land Lot 1270 in the 3rd District, 1st Section. Assuming power of attorney for owner John Dyson, Jacob Scudder had been instrumental in selling the lot to the Inferior Court of Forsyth County for $500 for use as the county seat after Forsyth County was created from Cherokee County in December 1832. With the establishment of a county government came the immediate need for a location to hold court. A temporary solution was the utilization of the home of William Hammond for the first sessions of Superior Court and Inferior Court. Then, a log courthouse was constructed. According to the late Garland Bagley, the first courthouse built by the county was on city lots 19 and 46 at the southwest corner of the square, which was on the right of Maple Street going west. This was a log courthouse built by the Andoe family in 1835.

Early county officials, who began serving in these modest buildings include: Oliver Strickland, clerk of the Superior Court; John Blaylock, clerk of the

Inferior Court; Isaac Wharton, Richard Hays, William Mathis, Mason Ezelle, and Absolum Reese, justices of the Inferior Court; Thomas Burford, surveyor; Alston B. Welborn, coroner; John Jolly, sheriff; Alexander Flanagan, tax collector; John R.Light, tax receiver; John W. Hooper, judge; and William H. Ray, clerk of the Court of Ordinary.

One building followed another. Forsyth County Historian Don Shadburn cited this quote by Mary Jane Patterson, who wrote:

> The first courthouse was built of logs and stood on the lot across from the jail. This served until 1839 when a large frame house was built in the center of the public square. In 1854 this building was rolled out to the southwest corner of the square and a brick house built which served until 1905 when the present structure was built.

According to Shadburn, the frame courthouse in the center of the town square apparently deteriorated rapidly. The April 1853 Grand Jury requested that the Inferior Court move the structure to the south side of the square and begin the construction of a new brick courthouse. On July 11, 1853, the frame building was sold to John W. McAfee for $177.50. Then, on November 18, 1853, Eratus Guild was hired to erect the new brick building. Payments on the building totaled $5,120 by its completion on July 22, 1854.

Like the first courthouse, the first jail was also a log structure built by the Andoe family—on town lot No. 82. In May 1866, this jail was accidentally burned and another was erected on the same site. A new jail was again needed in 1883 to be erected at a different location, a committee having determined that the old site was inadequate. Thus, on June 15, 1883, a contract was signed between William D. Bentley, commissioner of roads and revenues, and Joseph D. Foster to construct a masonry jail under the following specifications:

> 38 feet long by 28 feet wide according to outside measurements with veranda seven feet wide by 26 feet long and said building to be two stories high; the foundation to be built of rough stone reaching down to and resting upon rock or firm clay, said foundation to be two feet in width and extending 18 inches above the surface of the ground. The stones laid in strong mortar, the foundation provided with ventilation holes every six feet in length and breadth of same. The walls of the lower department of said jail are to be built laid in standard mortar of fresh lime and sharp sand thoroughly mixed . . .

The specifications continued on with every item explicitly detailed and the cost for this structure was $3,100.

The 1883 jail, which should have served the county for years, was destroyed by "accidental arson" on April 1, 1892. According to an article in the *Baptist Leader*, a white man, John Hall, was incarcerated for selling whiskey. Two

African-American men had been in detention for a longer period. These men had been boring and chiseling with tools left in the hallway by workmen constructing an iron cage when their bit broke and they gave up the thought of escape. Hall then seized upon an idea for escape himself and took the wood chips left from the chiseling activity and set them afire, ostensibly to burn a large enough hole to crawl through. Soon, however, the fire was beyond the control of the prisoners and they were forced to call for assistance. Sheriff Strickland managed to remove the three, but could save little of the jail property. The newspaper bemoaned the fact that the jail had cost $3,700 and an additional $800 for the iron cage and speculated that the three prisoners would likely be taken to Gainesville, Canton, or Marietta for safekeeping.

Forsyth County's first brick courthouse was built in 1854 and served the county until it was replaced by another brick structure in 1905.

4. Townships and Communities

Frogtown? One of the earliest and most densely populated areas in the settlement of the county was officially listed as Hightower on an 1847 map of Forsyth County. Frogtown, as the vicinity was popularly called, and nearby Ophir in Cherokee County, were the setting for extensive gold mining activity. Their locations along the trade route known as the Federal Road allowed settlers and prospectors ready access to this northwestern section of Forsyth County and eastern Cherokee. (The only other communities listed on the 1847 map by William H. Bonner were Hartford, later known as Oscarville, Vickery Creek, Big Creek, and Warsaw.)

With the pulse of the county emanating from its communities, it is prudent to take a close look at their growth and development. So sparse was the population of the county when the 1840 United States Census was enumerated that the data was included in one report. The numbers did increase, however, and, by 1870, the census was organized by districts: Big Creek, Hightower, Chestatee, Coal Mountain, Cumming, Borough of Cumming, Vickery Creek, and Chattahoochee.

A smaller community than Hightower or Frogtown to the northwest, Cumming, centrally located within Forsyth County, developed at a more leisurely pace probably because there were no established roads nearby. Nevertheless, Cumming had been incorporated as the county seat and eventually the town, chartered by the legislature in 1834, developed into an agricultural trading center that served the needs of an agrarian county as well as functioning as a government and justice center for the area.

For whom was Cumming named? The official position declares the town was named in honor of Colonel William Cumming of Augusta, born in 1788, a lawyer who had gained prominence in the war of 1812 and subsequently engaged in a series of duels with Senator George McDuffie of South Carolina over states' rights.

British specialists in place names promote a different story, however, and a different individual. Their *Dictionary of National Biography* claims that Sir Alexander Cumming of Aberdeen went to the United States in 1729 and established himself among the Native Americans. In 1730, Sir Alexander transported several Cherokees back to England with him, where they signed a friendship pact with

Ellene Strickland Kemp is pictured in an unusually heavy snow in Cumming. The daughter of Dr. Ansel Strickland, an early physician in Cumming, Kemp lived most of her life near the home where she was raised.

the British. Cumming was later credited with influencing the Cherokees to remain loyal to the British in the War of 1812.

For whom the town was really named had little to do with its growth and character through the years. The first account of Cumming's development was found in the papers of long-time resident J.G. Puett:

> The town of Cumming was first laid out by the Inferior Court of Forsyth County in 1833. No specific limit of its territory seems to have been fixed for the town until 1834, when it was incorporated by the General Assembly of the State. The work of the Inferior Court consisted of laying out the public square and blocking off the territory, prescribing streets and alleys and numbering the lots commencing at the southeast corner and numbering north, four lots fronting on the square; then number the next range around the square in the same way until the four blocks fronting on the square were all numbered. The first settlers in the town were: Nimrod Pendley, General Ira R. Foster, Richard Lester, Daniel Smith, William Staggs, William Blankinship, Jessie Stanley, Noah Strong, William Ray, Oliver Strickland, Hill Samuel Paxton, W.B. Hutchens, and Randall McDaniel.

The first church built in the town was a Baptist Church about the year 1838—a frame building which stood to the west of the Cumming Cemetery between the dwelling now occupied by Mr. Redd and the blacksmith Henry Brown. The Baptists have their third church building. . . . The next church built was a Methodist Church—built where it now stands about the year 1840.

Cumming, for a number of years, was noted for the manufacture of tobacco and cigars.

An article which appeared in the *Forsyth County News* on September 14, 1911, is signed "A Citizen" and reflects the agricultural center that was Cumming in the early years of the twentieth century:

A town situated in the hills of North Georgia, with about 435 inhabitants, and about seven miles of main streets, not including back streets and alleys. Two banks doing a good business, three dry goods stores, six grocery stores including those who handle dry goods in connection with their groceries. Four sales stables, two feed and livery stables, three wagon and buggy stores; three hay and grains stores, two harness stores, three furniture stores, three millinery parlors, four medical doctors, two drug stores, two blacksmith shops, one hotel and two boarding houses, four churches, two school buildings, three different places to sell fertilizers,

This Settendown school group is typical of the student bodies at the various community schools. Pupils ranged in age and size from five or six years old to almost grown.

two undertaker establishments, one door, sash, and cabinet shop, four places where you can buy farm implements, machinery, pumps, barbed wire and most anything you want in the hardware line. One oil mill and guano factory together with a public ginnery, one corn mill, one tannery, one harness shop, one shoe shop, one meat market, fifteen automobiles and one garage, one post office, one telephone exchange, two barber shops, one jewelry store, two printing offices—all this and more within the incorporate limits of Cumming.

Simultaneously with the development of Cumming, communities were springing up throughout the county. One such community was known as Settendown. In the early days, its location was noted as being 4 miles northwest of Cumming, 18 miles from Duluth, and 45 miles from Atlanta. With a population of 125, the area received mail tri-weekly. The nearest bank was in the town of Gainesville in Hall County. Citizens of the community included W.M. Bruce, millwright; W.L. Chamblee, postmaster and general store operator; William Dean, mason; Reverend A. Sheffield, Baptist minister; J.E. Smith, physician; W.H. Smith, cotton gin operator; William Tanner, millwright; and Wallace Trobble [Tribble?] and Company, gin and sawmill operators.

In a *Georgia State Gazetteer* of 1883–1884, Settendown was described as "Located on a creek of the same name, yielding abundant power; four miles northwest of Cumming, the seat of justice . . . has Baptist church, two common schools, and two steam gins." This listing mentioned the above citizens and added: Spears and Company, sawmill; D.C. Tallent, millwright; and farmers J.W. Edwards, W. Phillips, G.W. Reid, A.N. Tribble, J.W. Tribble, and J.B. Wallace.

Near Settendown was Coal Mountain. An interesting fact about this community was that they moved it. Literally. And there never was any coal either. Coal Mountain was originally located in the Six Mile Creek vicinity. Then, when William P. Garrett served as postmaster between the years 1891 and 1897, the post office was shifted west to the intersection of present-day State Routes 9 and 369. At its new site, a school and church—Mount Moriah—were established.

In 1892, the *Baptist Leader*, extolling the virtues of various religious institutions, published the following on a later church and the community that it served:

> This church [Coal Mountain Baptist] was organized October 21, 1886, without any house or place to worship, with only a few members. Most of the members came out from Mount Moriah Church nearby on account of the division among Baptists at that time. They soon built a good house, costing over $600, and have now a membership of 154 members. They had an increase last year of about 60 members, under the charge of Rev. J.B. Blackwell. Rev. A. B. Nuckolls was their first pastor, Rev. W.J. Hyde next and then Bro. Blackwell.
>
> The church is located in a beautiful section of the country and convenient of access, being at the crossing of the Cumming and

Dahlonega and Federal roads and level country all around. It is named after a spur of Sawnee Mountain, which runs northeast near the church, through the county. Coal Mountain is the name of the Post Office, in a few hundred yards of the church, and is almost a town.

Another Baptist and Methodist Church are in sight, Odd Fellow hall, and shops close by. About 250 inhabitants are living not far from the church. Dr. T.L. Lipscomb, who is a distinguished physician and member of the church, is located here and does a large practice. . . . Brother W.F. Wofford's doors are always open to the servants of Christ, to spend the night at his home nearly two miles west of the church.

To the southeast of Cumming lay Haw Creek, so dubbed for the haw bushes that adhered tenaciously to its banks. Residents of Forsyth County a few decades past remember traveling from Cumming and heading east on Highway 20 at the Buford Crossing—the intersection of Highways 9 and 20—which was marked by one lone service station. From this crossing, an individual need only have traveled a short distance on Highway 20 before reaching Haw Creek.

Gone now is the rural scene of our traveler's destination. Rolling hills, where animals grazed and crops and farmhouses rounded out the pastoral setting, have been replaced by businesses and homes on postage-stamp lots. To say that the traditional community has completely vanished would be a misstatement, for family names such as Anglin, Barrett, Benefield, Blackstock, Cook, Day, Echols, Fowler, Garner, Gilbert, Green, Hansard, Major, Payne, Vaughan, and Wood, are still currently associated with the area. Granted though, William Barker, who was the Haw Creek postmaster in 1878, would not be able to identify with the postage-stamp lots and commercial enterprises of today. In retrospect, one questions, "where have all the haw bushes gone?"

One of the few vestiges of the old community is Haw Creek Baptist Church with its cemetery dating back to the early days of Forsyth County. The church having been founded in 1841, Haw Creek's charter members included: William Blackstock, Hannah Blackstock, Delilah Phillips, Richard Phillips, Perthane Phillips, Healin Phillips, Alsey Wright, William Vaughan, Clinton Vaughan, Delilah Vaughan, Asa Vaughan, Willis Vaughan, Hannah Vaughan, and Louisa Russell. Ten years later, in 1851, the church was dissolved only to be reorganized in 1856 by R. Phillips, Neamon C. Nicholson, James Major Sr., Norman C. Nicholson, Dilly Phillips, S.J. Nicholson, Lewis B. Phillips, and Clarinda Major.

Haw Creek Baptist Church doubtless played the most prominent role in the life of the community, but Haw Creek School's influence also elevated the future of its pupils. In 1916, the teachers were Maude and Bell Hughes.

Moving to the northeastern section of the county, one may pass through Oscarville, once called Hartford. A few years back, natives of the county would have 'lowed that it was located "over towards Gainesville." To augment that nonspecific answer, one may depart slightly from the movie title *A River Runs Through It* and declare that a highway runs through it—State Route 369—and, once, a river was a prominent feature of the area. Now, Lake Lanier has not only replaced the Chattahoochee River, but displaced numerous family farms in the vicinity as well.

The unique character of the community and its history is found in its institutions, its people, and events—natural and human—which shaped the development of the land once occupied by the Cherokees and, in the late 1700s and early 1800s, dominated by Chief James Vann. The site of Vann's Tavern is now under the waters of Lake Sidney Lanier, but a reminder of its existence remains in the form of a nearby recreation area appropriately named "Vann's Tavern Park."

In addition to the local farms and agrarian enterprises such as the Reynolds' blacksmith shop, Oscarville was comprised of two churches, two stores, and a community school. Crow's Store and Orr's Store served the needs of an agricultural way of life. From farming implements and seeds for spring planting to wares the farmers' wives could not produce by their own labor, the country store was an institution unto itself.

Education, too, was important to the citizens of the area, as evidenced by the attendance at Mt. Zion School. Families represented in 1916 included Green, Watson, Bennett, Crow, Waldrip, Durand, Dover, Jordan, Mathis, Olivet, Jordan, Murphy, Hale, Hemphill, Reed, Ledbetter, Bond, Smith, Bryson, and Booker.

Across the road from the school once stood Mt. Zion Methodist Church. Little is known of the church history. Only a membership list, located in the records

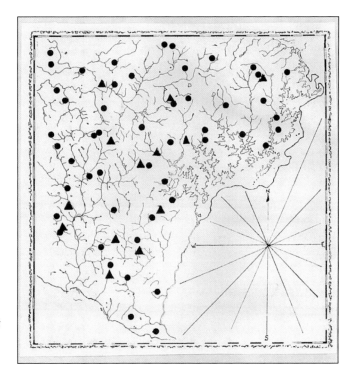

On this map of Forsyth County Schools by Steve Conrad, the circles represent schools of the past, while the triangles indicate current institutions. Locations are approximate.

Oscarville was one of the county's agrarian communities. In 1929, Charlie Freeland, Clarence Waldrip, and Hoyt Freeland were pictured harvesting oats with an old fashioned cradle.

of New Hope Methodist Church, is extant. Reading like a partial census of the community, this roll named the following families in the community: Bailey, Bennett, Boyd, Cantrell, Chambers, Close, Crumbley, Gipson, Gober, Hadder, Harris, Harwell, Hope, Jordan, Manns, Massey, McConnell, McHugh, Mooney, Morgan, Padgett, Props, Puckett, Scroggins, Smith, Starks, Stewart, Stroud, Summers, Swofford, Tanner, Tate, Timms, Turner, Whitmire, Williams, Winn, Woodliff, and others. Neither Mt. Zion School nor Mt. Zion Methodist Church still stand today, but the church cemetery bears testimony to those who lived, worked, and died near Oscarville. Two of the earliest families buried there were the Williams and Woodliffs.

Not all institutions have vanished from the community however, for Mt. Zion Lodge #316 Free and Accepted Masons, chartered on October 28, 1885, remains one of the most active Masonic lodges in the county. Moreover, Pleasant Grove Baptist Church, established in 1872, continues to be a strong influence in Oscarville. When organized in 1872, the church had approximately 30 members, many of whom erected the first building of logs with their own hands. On January 8, 1881, the first recorded conference was held with B.H. Brown as moderator and O. Clark as clerk.

In the church yard adjoining the present fine brick structure lie the graves of scores of early settlers, as well as later members. Of note, Mae Crow, rape victim of 1912, is interred with other members of the Crow family. Born on September

16, 1893, Mae Crow succumbed on September 23, 1912 to injuries suffered a few days earlier. Another nearby house of worship, Silver Shoals Baptist Church, constituted in 1886, remains active today.

The area may be extended to include Brown's Bridge and Two Mile Creek. In an article of undetermined date and publication, Sybil McRay of Gainesville once quoted a piece dating to the early 1900s by G.H. Bell of Oakwood in which the author described the community commencing at Brown's Bridge:

> Just across the river on the Forsyth side stands the old Brown mansion, the home of Minor Brown during ante-bellum days, and later occupied by Hon. Oliver Clark, who represented Forsyth County in the Constitution Convention of 1877. (Minor Brown later moved to Gainesville and Oliver Clark once lived in Hall County.) This is a large two-story house with box chimneys and surrounded by a grove of large walnut, locust, and water oaks. Across the public road is the storehouse where at one time a large mercantile business was carried on. Nearby is the home place of Bes___ Allen.
>
> Passing on, we next come to Oscarville (old Morgantown) where there is a large school building, Masons and Oddfellow Hall, and two churches.
>
> There is also at this place two stores and a large ginnery. This is the old home place of the late Rev. Crawford C. Morgan, a Methodist minister, who during the 1880s conducted a large tannery nearby. About a mile further after crossing Two Mile Creek, there is the old Green place (later known as the Otwell place). This was settled by the late James A. Green, who was before and during the War Between the States, principal keeper of the Georgia penitentiary at Milledgeville.

The fate of nearby Brown's Bridge is a story unto itself, with natural disasters destroying span after span, but Brown's Bridge was not the only span to encounter disaster. An iron bridge located to its south met with a similar fate, but this was man-made. In a 1984 interview with Julianne Boling, resident Toma Reynolds, then 95 years old, recalled the bridge that connected the Oscarville area to Flowery Branch. She declared that now, because of Lake Lanier, the distance is much farther. And what happened to the iron bridge? An effort was made to save the span that traversed the Chattahoochee, but, as luck would have it, after it was purchased and plans were underway to move it to safety, the waters of Lake Lanier rose so quickly that it was inundated before it could be shifted to a different site. In pondering the demise of the bridge, one might be led to wonder: if the lake is lowered to satisfy future water needs, will the bridge once again be visible? After all, it's down there!

From Oscarville, go west, young man—and you will arrive at Matt. Matt community was named for Madison Martin and was sometimes called Mat on maps and official records. But that was later. Before its name was changed to Matt, the post office was called Omega and was located on Land Lot 384 in the 3rd District, 1st Section of the county just four miles west of Coal Mountain. James H. Barrett, the first commissioned postmaster, served from December 19, 1893 until W.A. Holbrook assumed the duties on June 26, 1895. Holbrook could claim the title for only five months however, as Omega Post Office was discontinued and the mail routed briefly through Coal Mountain.

A few months after the demise of Omega, or at least until the discontinuance of the name, a new post office, established on the same land lot, was known as Matt. The new postmaster was not a new postmaster at all, but W.A. Holbrook, who resumed his old capacity on May 5, 1896. Holbrook must have had difficulty remembering whether he was postmaster at any given time, for the post office was discontinued on October 17, 1903 with the mail sent to Cumming, and then re-established on March 31, 1904 with—not hard to guess—W.A. Holbrook as postmaster. During his tenure in the office, Holbrook was authorized to issue money orders beginning on July 14, 1905. The final postmaster for Matt was to be Ulysses G. Blanton, who held the title from September 18, 1907 until the post office was discontinued permanently on February 28, 1911.

About four decades later, the Community Improvement Club at Matt issued a few concise statements concerning the post office, which differed from the official records cited above, and of the area's unique characteristics:

> Matt community was once Omega. Because another Post Office in the state [claimed] that name, it was changed to Matt. It was named for Madison Martin, whose son was Postmaster at that time. . . . Mail was delivered on foot three times per week.
>
> There we had a one-room teacher school [with] about 75 pupils well under control; no desks, slabs for seats, and an open fireplace; spring water to drink; no school buses or any automobiles. Some scholars walked two to four miles.
>
> Their farming was done with a bull tongue plow pulled by a mule or horse and one acre per day was good breaking up, and two acres per day, extra running around. Most men cut one to two cords of wood per day at not over $1.00 per cord.
>
> Zion Hill Church was a wood[en] unpainted house; no arbor, no piano; song books usually had no music—preacher read words, congregation sang them. All went in wagons, road carts, or rode mules or went often three to five miles on foot.

Education for the community began in an old wooden schoolhouse on Elmo Road in close proximity to Hurt and Moore's Store (on the site of the present Leon's). Grades 1-9 were taught at "Matt High School," as it was called, until the crude building was destroyed by fire in 1942. Subsequently, students attended classes at Zion Hill Baptist Church while the new brick school on Bannister Road was under construction. Students were divided into two groups; the younger

Maggie Worley taught at Matt School until the school was consolidated in 1968. She subsequently finished her career at Sawnee Elementary.

pupils were taught by Maggie Worley, while older students were under the charge of Louise Walls.

The core of any community is its religious institution and Matt's Zion Hill Church was no exception. Providing for the religious needs of citizens in the vicinity, Zion Hill offered the strength to mold the moral fiber of its members and the sustenance to see those same individuals through the difficulties of life. Constituted in 1881, Zion Hill continues to serve the Matt community.

Matt might have stayed the same fairly self-contained agricultural burg with its citizens trading at Hurt and Moore's or Grogan's stores, attending the local church and school, and enduring the hard times that were the aftermath of the Great Depression but for two forces that forever changed the community.

The first was a switch in cash crops. With cotton reaching an all-time low on the world market, the farmers could not follow tradition and sustain their families at the same time. Thus, when the chance to raise a more lucrative "crop" appeared, families began growing chickens. And, with the advent of the poultry industry, the standard of living rose in the next few years. The paving of Highway 369 was another community-altering factor. A paved road was more than a mere convenience. Indeed, it speeded up the pace of life at Matt and that pace has not slowed since.

By mid–century, Matt was ripe for other changes, too. These came in the form of the activities of the Community Improvement Club, which lived up to its name. To contrast the living conditions of earlier times with what followed is truly a lesson in what can be accomplished with increased capital and the will of the people to improve their lot in life: The "old" Matt evidenced numerous unattractive homes, unlandscaped school grounds, red clay gullies, a school with no lunchroom, eroded farm and pasture land, neglected yards, and an out-dated church building. Sound bleak? It was fixable. The Community Improvement Club scrapbook described the changes:

> Now [1950s], thanks to the Community Improvement Club, the school grounds have been landscaped, grass sown, and cement walks made. The children are now enjoying hot lunches in the modern up-to-date lunchroom and tile has been purchased to put on the floors. Many acres of pasture land have been sown and farm land has been improved greatly with proper terracing, manure from chicken houses, and planting of legumes. The church has been replaced with a modern brick structure and new benches, and the grounds are beautiful with shrubbery and flowers. The homes and yards have been improved greatly.

Friendship Baptist Church provided for the religious needs of the citizens in the settlement known as Cuba. This photo was snapped from the cemetery across the road, then a section of the Cumming-Canton Highway.

About 5 miles south of Matt and four miles west of Cumming lies the Friendship community. Friendship Baptist Church was constituted in 1840 and school buildings also called Friendship existed in the settlement known as Cuba—named for a card game residents played—as well as agricultural businesses and Ben Roper's Store, the site of his fatal attack in 1943. Later Roper's daughter Alyce Redd operated a store nearby.

Panning to the westernmost section of the county, along the border with Cherokee, the area later incorporated as Ducktown was first known as Harmony. On March 15, 1891, a post office was established on Land Lot 867 in the 3rd District, 1st Section of Forsyth County with John W. Hawkins serving as postmaster. This post office was served by Route 15199 from Cumming to Orange (located in Cherokee County). Because there was another Harmony in the state of Georgia and mail frequently became routed to the wrong location, the name was changed to Ducktown on October 5, 1899 with John W. Hawkins remaining as postmaster. On October 26, 1901, Lewis Ledbetter became postmaster and was later commissioned. Ducktown Post Office was discontinued on October 17, 1903, effective October 31, 1903, and mail was sent to the Cumming Post Office.

Tradition holds that the name Ducktown derived from a flock of ducks that roamed the town and would follow patrons to various businesses when they traded in the vicinity.

Ducktown, in the early twentieth century, was a thriving community as evidenced by efforts to incorporate the "business district." Approval for the incorporation of Ducktown was granted by the Georgia legislature on August 9, 1912; hence, Ducktown became a municipality. Other than Cumming, Ducktown has been the only incorporated township in Forsyth County.

Lewis T. Ledbetter served as mayor of Ducktown for a number of years and operated a general store at the crossroads. Ledbetter, at age 41, was listed in the draft of 1917 and 1918 for World War I. He later served as superintendent of construction when Rural Electrification Association (REA) brought electricity to area farmers. Lewis Ledbetter (born December 24, 1876, died October 8, 1971) and wife Loma C. (born March 2, 1878, died June 28, 1950) are both buried nearby in New Harmony Baptist Church cemetery. The *Forsyth County News* from January 18, 1923, reported the results of the election for the municipal officers of Ducktown: M.L. Howard, Mayor; Sam Sandow, Assistant Mayor; and J.W. Lummus, G.A. Ledbetter, and J.W. Miller, Councilmen.

During the early days of its incorporation, Ducktown was a bustling area, with the town providing for the needs of an agrarian community. In addition to Ledbetter's store, a cotton warehouse, blacksmith shop, mule barn, and jail were at the hub of the town and houses dotting the surrounding property. New Harmony Baptist Church, located a short distance from the center of town, provided for the religious needs of the municipality. This bustling township, however, did not continue to thrive. When the cotton warehouse and other structures burned, the town never fully recovered from the economic loss. Then, in the mid–1940s, the highway from Cumming to Canton was not only paved, but rerouted somewhat. Ducktown was no longer on the main road, and the development of highway businesses shifted to the new location.

Ducktown was not the only location to acquire an unusual name, for "Jot 'em Down" in the Chestatee area of northern Forsyth may be able to best even Ducktown in the name department. How did this community become Jot 'em Down and what distinguishing features did it possess decades ago? To answer the first part of the question, one must examine a bit of radio history, for the name Jot 'em Down was adopted from the Lum and Abner radio program of the 1930s. According to the script for the show, the program originated from Jot 'em Down General Store in the village of Pine Ridge, Arkansas. True to life in the Depression days, when cash was almost nonexistent and farmers depended on credit for survival, a farmer would enter the store, select the necessary items, and instruct the storekeeper to "jot 'em down" on his account to be paid when and if the farmer's crops were harvested and sold. At any rate, when the farmers gathered at the store at this particular intersection in Forsyth County, they frequently lingered long enough to hear the Lum and Abner broadcast. Then, at some point, the store took the name Jot 'em Down and the surrounding area assumed that designation as well.

A description of Jot 'em Down (in Forsyth County) from the 1930s and 1940s era proves as unique as the name itself. The roads of the early days were unpaved and they seemed to respect stately old trees; in this instance, one massive oak. In the center of the intersection stood a grand old tree, unmolested in the name of "progress" save for a wooden sign attached to its trunk—a picture of a hand with a turtle firmly attached to one finger and lettered with the admonition "I got bit by not trading with W.H. Hammond." It is uncertain how many folks heeded the sign and traded with Hammond's Store at another intersection, but all did, however, maneuver around the tree as they negotiated the intersection. Unfortunately, the oak tree in the intersection is gone now and in its place is a traffic light. No turtles have been spotted recently.

The business enterprises of the community developed in the 1930s. Long-time Forsyth Countian George Welch remembers that Barney Pendley moved a small store from the Clayton Daniel property a short distance from the east side of the intersection to the corner where the present building, known today as Jot 'em Down Store, is located. Another resident, Walter Porter, added that mules and poles were employed to transport the little store about one mile from its original site around the year 1930. The move having been accomplished, Pendley added living quarters to the back of the structure and later sold the store to Paul and Voncille Chastain Porter, who had married in April 1935. At once, Paul Porter was a popular merchant, as he boasted the first radio in the community. Residents convened on a regular basis to listen to their favorite programs—one, of course, being Lum and Abner.

Jot 'em Down Store has passed through a number of owner/operators throughout its years of serving the community. These individuals include Barney Pendley, Paul Porter, Grady Watson, and Mark Porter, who ran the business until his death in 1962, at which time his wife Vernell took over for a time. Mark and Vernell Porter's daughter Barbara finally sold out after the general store had been under Porter management for approximately 50 years.

A few years after the Jot 'em Down Store was established, Adrian Bennett erected a warehouse and feed store just across the road from the general store, thus replacing a barn that had graced the intersection for years. Then, D.O. Freeman took over operations and the building became a chicken feed store as farmers turned from raising cotton to growing "hot house" chickens. Later still, the structure, which catty-cornered on the intersection, became Freeman's grocery. Freeman and family resided in a house on the west side of the store on present-day Highway 306.

Within walking distance to the north, the dirt road (Jot 'em Down Road) passed through what was locally called "Dry Pond." Actually, Dry Pond was more of a phenomenon than a specific site, but try to tell that to the person who had to drive through in rainy weather and found his car stuck in the mud or drowned out in the "pond."

Crossing Highway 306 to the opposite side of the intersection, one finds the present Jot 'em Down Tire and Wheel where previously only woods could be seen. But the other corner, dominated by the new Amoco station, was the home of the Owen family. Spruill Owen, the fourth child of Wiley and Mary Quarles Owen, raised his family in the house, which was removed several years ago and an Amoco station built on the site.

Spruill Owen raised his family at the intersection dubbed Jot 'em Down. On two of the other corners were a general store and a chicken feed store.

The Settle family was prominent in the southeastern section. Pictured from left to right are (front row) Grady, Gert, Toy (baby), Ida, George T., Fred, Sara E., and (back row) Charles L. and Clarence Settle.

From north to southeast, the names Terry and Settles are synonymous with the growth and development of the Shakerag community. Martin Terry, born on January 5, 1816 in Tennessee, married Mary Dodd and raised a large family in southeastern Forsyth County. Upon Martin Terry's death, his wife inherited land in nine lots, including lot number 1079, which is the site of one of the oldest houses in the county. Subsequent to the death of Terry, the land passed through a series of owners. Finally, in 1892, George Thomas Settle and his wife Sarah Cottrell Settle purchased the property. Since Sarah was the granddaughter of Martin Terry, the name "Terry-Settle House" was established and the house remained in the Settle family for almost 100 years.

As the Terry and Settle families grew and prospered, their descendants, and members of the community as well, were amassing a wealth of fond memories of agrarian life in the days of yesteryear. The late Dorothy Terry Manning recalled her visits to the home of Ida and Toy Settle. Because her grandparents lived on the Bud Settle place, she would walk from there across the woods to the Terry-Settle House. But back then, it was just the home of "Mr. Toy" and "Miss Ida," brother and sister who made visitors welcome with mouth-watering treats from the kitchen and a chat on the cool, enclosed porch. Manning also remembered that her grandfather, Euel John Terry, made syrup at the mill on Toy and Ida Settle's farm.

The land owned by Toy Settle once contained approximately 264 acres situated along the meandering Chattahoochee River. Idyllic though the setting may have been, the river nevertheless posed an obstacle for those wishing to be on the other side. A ferry—Terry's Ferry—served to transport citizens to and fro on the river until 1915, when an iron bridge was erected to link Forsyth and Gwinnett Counties. Years later, in an interview with Scott Vaughan, Toy Settle described the preparations for the bridge. "We had to build the road on around to the narrow place [in the river] and make a circle so that people would have access to the bridge. We had to clear it out and make the road ourselves." Toy Settle couldn't explain, however, how the span came to be known as "Settle's Bridge." Incidentally, the total cost of the bridge was $4,750, with Forsyth County's part of the payment set at $1,500.

In addition to the communities described, others included on a 1920 map by the National Map Company were Silver City, Novetta, Arch, Mish, Storeville, Pleasant, Otis, Lane, Heardsville, Spot, Drew, Sevier, Liverpool, Odell, Itley, Nettie, Big Creek, and Gravel Springs. Throughout the county's history, communities have gone by different names, become part of nearby areas, and, in the case of southern Forsyth County, even merged into another county.

Settle's Bridge, connecting Forsyth and Gwinnett Counties, replaced the Terry Ferry across the Chattahoochee River.

5. Noted Individuals

The saga of Forsyth County is the story of her people. The lives of many of the outstanding individuals who helped shape the character of the area spanned numerous decades and, therefore, cannot be categorized into specific time periods. To begin, however, in the early days of the county, it is well to note that several Revolutionary soldiers migrated to Forsyth County and on to other regions of the country. Only John LeGrand settled in the county and remained until his death.

LeGrand was born on November 4, 1760 in Halifax County, Virginia and died *c.* 1843 in Forsyth County. He married Elizabeth Younger, born *c.* 1765 in Halifax County, Virginia, and Lucinda Christian on August 8, 1827 in Elbert County, Georgia. John LeGrand was the son of Abraham LeGrand, born *c.* 1724 in Herrico County, Virginia, and Agnes (Agathy) Nichols LeGrand.

Virtually all that has been gleaned from a National Archives search for data on LeGrand is that he served with the German Battalion, Continental Troops during the Revolution. On June 28, 1779, his name appeared on a return of the sick in the German Regiment of Lieutenant Colonel Weltner. His affliction was listed as "fever and gravel."

Decades passed and John LeGrand, then located in Nellum's District of Elbert County, Georgia, applied for land in the 1832 Cherokee Land Lottery of Georgia. First recorded in the Cherokee Land Lottery of Georgia by James F. Smith in 1838, the following entry was later included in the roster of Lucian Lamar Knight and in *Georgia Genealogical Reprints* by the Reverend Silas Emmett Lucas Jr.: "John LeGrand, Revolutionary Soldier, Nellum's, Elbert drew Land Lot 309 in the 24th District. 2nd Section of Cherokee."

By 1840, LeGrand was enumerated in the United States Census of Forsyth County, #273. The next year the aged soldier joined Friendship Baptist Church. The church minutes record for Saturday, November 20, 1841 reads: "Services were held at the home of John LeGrand [later the Johnny Watson property on McConnell Road] and afterward preaching by J.L. Hudson. Brother John LeGrand joined by experience at the age of 87 years and 16 days old. Toliver Reid, Church Clerk." LeGrand's membership at Friendship, however, lasted less than a year. He was carried to the creek and baptized at the end of revival

Revolutionary soldier John LeGrand was buried on the farm later owned by the Watson family. His grave was recently marked by the Sons of the American Revolution.

services in 1841, but church minutes indicate that he was dismissed by letter on August 28, 1842.

When John LeGrand passed away, he was buried on the Thomas Redd place, land that would later be owned by Fred Watson and currently is owned by Delmer Watson. The spot was marked by field stones, while a walnut tree stood sentinel. Perhaps LeGrand's final resting place will best be remembered by Mrs. Fred Watson's casual reference to it as "some of St. Peter's folks," later shortened simply to "Peter's grave." In 2001, LeGrand's grave was marked in a ceremony by the Sons of the American Revolution.

Soldiers may have drawn land and settled in the former Cherokee nation, but the preachers were the devoted group that upheld moral principles in an untamed land. Alfred Webb is representative of those individuals—assisting in establishing churches throughout the area. When Webb passed away at an advanced age, his obituary paid tribute to the accomplishments and the character of the man:

> This venerable father in Christ "fell asleep" near Dawsonville, Georgia, Sunday, October 7 at the age of 83 years. A native of North Carolina, he came to our state nearly half a century ago, in the prime of life and in "the fullness of the blessing of the gospel." His faithful labors soon resulted in the constitution of four churches in Lumpkin [now Dawson], Forsyth and Cherokee counties, and to these he ministered

Alfred Webb was an effective Baptist leader who established several churches throughout the area, including Concord at Silver City.

in holy things until the infirmities of age compelled him to cease from his "loved employ" on their behalf. For over forty years his brethren of the Hightower Association called him to the position of Moderator, and recognized him as a leader alike in their councils and their toils. In many respects he ranks among the most remarkable men who have ever lived in North Georgia.

One of the churches that Alfred Webb helped establish was Concord Baptist in the Silver City community. In 1892, the *Baptist Leader* indicated that Concord was constituted in 1837 or 1838 under a shade tree on the road leading from Nuckolsville to Frogtown, near where James Cox resided. The presbytery consisted of Reverend Alfred Webb, moderator; Abraham Beam, deacon and secretary; Johnson Ledbetter, deacon; and Reverend Bailey Bruce and Reverend William Mears. Of Webb, it was recorded that he "was called to the care of the church and has been regularly called as pastor every succeeding year to the present [1892]."

Interestingly, Concord Baptist Church was first established as a campground about a mile north of the Forsyth County line. A short time later, the church was either given or secured Land Lot number 41 in the 3rd District, 1st Section of Forsyth County for the sum of $5 at a sheriff's sale. Several church buildings have existed on this property, which is still the site of Concord Baptist Church today.

From minister to lay person, another early Forsyth Countian was equally as distinguished in the areas of his calling. Plantation owner, gold miner, public servant—Hardy Strickland was a pioneer settler of special note. Arriving with his sister Nancy Strickland Harrell and brothers Oliver, Tolbert, and Henry, Hardy made his home in the newly-created county prior to 1835. As a pioneer in the former Cherokee territory, he exerted his influence in determining the course of events that the county and, indeed, the state of Georgia would follow for the next several decades. From the records of Julia Strickland Looper, dated September 26, 1929, comes the following account of Hardy Strickland:

> At an early age he left his native Jackson County and made his home in Forsyth County. Here he engaged with his brother Henry Strickland in the mining for gold. They operated what is now known as the "Strickland Old Mine" in Forsyth County for a number of years. They mined large quantities of gold which they had coined at the mint in Dahlonega.
>
> While superintending the mine he was unanimously nominated to represent Forsyth in the legislature; was elected and served in the House and Senate 16 years. He was not in Cumming at the time of his nomination and knew nothing of the contemplated action of the convention. The honor was unsought.

Concord Baptist Church was first established as a campground. The building pictured is one of several utilized by the congregation through the years.

Hardy Strickland served in the Georgia House of Representatives from 1847 to 1848 and 1849 to 1850. A few years later, he became Forsyth County's State Senator, holding the position from 1853 to 1854, 1855 to 1856, and 1857 to 1858.

Strickland progressed from an outstanding figure in the Georgia legislature, where he served intermittently from 1847 to 1858, to an active participant in regional politics. With war imminent, Strickland became an influential delegate from Forsyth County to Georgia's secession convention in Milledgeville. Both he and Colonel Hiram P. Bell had been unanimously chosen to represent Forsyth County at this convention, which voted for the ordinance of secession on January 19, 1861.

Months later, Strickland, acting on his convictions, enlisted in the Confederate cavalry and rushed forth into battle in the Civil War, but his military service was to be short-lived, for his skills were needed in the Confederate Congress. Strickland, representing the Ninth District of Georgia, served in the First Confederate Congress in Richmond, Virginia from February 18, 1862 to February 17, 1864. Suffering from rheumatism, he declined reelection, but again entered the military. Joining the state troops, he was appointed quartermaster for his brigade, a position he held until the war drew to a close in 1865.

Like fellow southerners, Strickland was virtually penniless at the conclusion of the hostilities. Yet, he industriously sought to adapt to new conditions and endeavored to develop the agricultural and mineral resources of the region.

He spent his last years as a resident of Acworth, Georgia, where he passed away in 1884 and was laid to rest in Liberty Hill Cemetery. Born December 3, 1828, his wife Eliza died January 1, 1897 and was buried beside him. The tombstone of Hardy Strickland is inscribed thusly:

> HARDY STRICKLAND
> BORN 11-24-1818
> DIED 1-24-1884
> HE SERVED 14 YEARS IN THE HOUSE OF REPRESENTATIVES AND SENATE OF GEORGIA, WAS A MEMBER OF THE CONFEDERATE CONGRESS. A MAN OF INTEGRITY OF PRINCIPLE AND HIGH SENSE OF HONOR. A KIND AND TENDER HUSBAND, BRIGHT AND HOPEFUL UNDER LONG AND INTENSE SUFFERING.

Plantation owners such as Hardy Strickland and farmers alike, depended on millwrights as an integral part of the agricultural system. Kelly Mill Road, extending a short distance from west of the Cumming square to Vickery Creek, led to the mill of Andrew Jackson Kelly, who operated the enterprise on a large tract of land that once contained the improvements of Cherokee Chief Sawnee at the base of what is known as Sawnee Mountain. Winnie Bramblett Tallant wrote the following of Andrew Jackson Kelly:

> Andy Kelly went to California during the 50s Gold Rush along with James W. Tribble, Absolem Wingo and a Chadwick man. He served his

country during the War between the States as a private in the Cherokee Repellers Company D. He enlisted at Shiloh, Cherokee County and was discharged in Rome, Georgia.

Early in the 1870s he moved to Cumming. He bought 500 acres of land, built a flour mill—which he operated for many years. He built a large two-story house for his family on a hill just above the mill.

Dr. Marcus Mashburn, Sr. recalled the following incident in his church history at the Cumming Methodist Church Homecoming in 1953: "I can remember there was a little road in front of the church and the old Heavenbush tree that stood at some distance between the church and the road. In my mind's eye I can see brother Andy Kelly as he drove his yellow mule to a side spring buggy and hitched it to that tree and went in to worship. If the preacher preached longer than two hours, this old mule would begin braying. Since I was quite a child then, and as now, not interested in too long a sermon, I almost felt like joining in the chorus."

Andrew Jackson Kelly died in November 1906 and was laid to rest in Cumming Cemetery.

Hiram Bell was a versatile individual—soldier, Mason, author, lawyer, and statesman—who served in the Confederate Congress and the United States Congress.

Abijah Julian could best be described as a public servant. He served in the Georgia legislature and in various capacities as a community leader.

Another Cumming citizen, Colonel R.P. Lester, was also revered by those who knew him. Born in Lawrenceville, Gwinnett County on November 30, 1832, Colonel Lester spent his boyhood and teen years in Cumming, where he married Mary J. Waddell on November 1, 1855. Lester was just becoming established as a successful lawyer when the Civil War began in 1861. A southern patriot to the core, he raised a company of volunteers and was elected captain. From that position, in the 14th Georgia Regiment, Company E, he was promoted in regular gradations to the rank of colonel and was in command of the 14th Georgia Regiment at the surrender at Appomattox in 1865.

Back home in Cumming after the war, Colonel Lester again engaged in the practice of law. When Lester passed away on November 29, 1902, his obituary in the *North Georgian* stated the following:

> Col. Lester was a gallant confederate soldier, was prominent in Masonic circles . . . and for 50 years he was a consistent member of the Methodist church . . . Col. Lester was never a candidate for any office, but took a deep interest in public affairs and always took a decided stand on the right side on all questions of public interest.

Perhaps Cumming and Forsyth County's most distinguished citizen was Colonel Hiram Parks Bell. The son of Joseph Scott Bell and Rachael Phinazee Bell, Hiram Bell was born on January 19, 1827 in Jackson County, Georgia. Young Bell attended school in Cumming and, in 1850, married Virginia Margaret Lester and settled in Cumming, where he practiced law and assumed an active role in community affairs. Author, Mason, orator, Civil War soldier, and state senator, Colonel Bell gained further renown as a leader by serving in both the Confederate Congress and the United States Congress.

Having lived a long and productive life, Hiram Parks Bell died on August 16, 1907, a few months after the publication of his volume *Men and Things*, in which he expounded on the history of Forsyth County, the South, politics, religion, the Civil War, and a multitude of other subjects.

Although no Civil War battles were fought in Forsyth County, nevertheless, the county raised its share of volunteers for the war for southern independence. None, however, could give a more captivating account of the realities of war than John Alvin Garrett. The following is a story related by Garrett and remembered by his grandson Dr. Rupert Bramblett:

> His vivid account of the Battle of Chickamauga would cause me to feel my hair standing on end, as he described the shooting, the smoke, screaming horses and screaming wounded men. I especially remember one scene which he described when the Confederate soldiers were in trenches they had dug on the hillside, as he described it, and the Yankees charging up the hill. He would say "Aye, God, they could never learn the range. They was shootin' up, and their bullets would hit the ground below us. We was aimin' down towards 'em and when it was over, I could have walked a mile, back and forth, on dead Yankee soldiers without ever steppin' on the ground."

When one thinks of Civil War soldiers and public servants, Abijah John Julian immediately comes to mind. Julian was only 16 years of age when his father died. His education was acquired in the county schools, a school in Gainesville, and in the Hearn Academy in Cave Springs, Georgia. He was but 19 years of age when war between the states was declared. He volunteered, joining the 43rd Georgia Infantry, in which he served for 16 months. He afterwards served a few months in Armstrong's Cavalry and was later transferred to General Joseph Wheeler's Company G, 1st Alabama Cavalry Regiment, in which he served until the end of the war, receiving his honorable discharge from the army in Charlotte, North Carolina on May 4, 1865.

On April 19, 1864, Julian married Minnie Bailey, daughter of Dr. Samuel S. and Julia A. Thompson Bailey, in Cherokee County, Alabama, where the Bailey family had refugeed during the Civil War.

Miscellaneous papers in the collection of the late Garland Bagley contained the following summary of Julian's political career:

Mr. Julian held during his lifetime many offices of trust. In 1872 he was appointed Justice of the Peace and served one year. He served four years as Representative of Forsyth County in the State Legislature, his first term beginning in 1880. In 1888, Julian was elected Senator from the 39th district . . . It was during this session that the new state capitol was finished.

In addition to his service in state government, Julian became a trustee of the Clarksville A&M School from the time of its establishment until his death in 1921. In 1901, he secured the first Rural Free Delivery in the 9th Congressional District for his area. Another area first, the rural telephone line to Gainesville, resulted from his efforts. For several years, he served as President of Wooley's Ford Telephone Company. Moreover, this industrious gentleman, as agent for Frick Engine Company, sold farm machinery, including the first steam and threshing machines in northeast Forsyth County.

Yet another Civil War soldier went on to a successful career: John C. Hallman, a businessman in Atlanta. Hallman resided in Cumming with his father George Washington Hallman at the onset of the Civil War. Slightly over 17 years old at the time, he enlisted in the Confederate Army and served with the Stonewall Jackson and A.P. Hill Corps in Company E, 14th Georgia Regiment, Wilcox's Division until he was furloughed in October 1863 after a skull fracture and paralysis incurred during the battle around Spottsylvania.

Subsequent to the war, Hallman was drawn to Atlanta and the business opportunities in the city abustle with reconstruction. Beginning in 1868, he took a prominent role in the development of Atlanta, first in the wholesale grocery business and then in the parent companies of the Georgia Power Company—Georgia Railway and Electric Company. In addition, he was a member of the board of directors of the Atlanta Title and Trust Company and a pioneer in developing transportation for the Atlanta area. Not only had he established a mule-car line from Broad Street out to West End, but he had built a small railway from West End to the gates of West View Cemetery, which he had helped organize when Atlanta's first major cemetery, Oakland, was rapidly becoming filled. Hallman, who married Isabella Henderson after the Civil War, was a member of the First Baptist Church and a faithful Democrat who voted in every election.

The next outstanding individual did not serve in the Civil War, but she is credited with a "first" in the State of Georgia. Born on June 24, 1859 in Forsyth County, Alice Harrell was the daughter of Newton and Mary Harris Harrell and the granddaughter of Nancy Strickland Harrell, one of the original settlers of Forsyth County. Harrell married her cousin, Henry Strickland Jr., a lawyer and businessman of Duluth, on November 10, 1889. The couple raised seven children who were achievers in their own right.

Described as "progressive," Alice Harrell Strickland was a community-minded woman who repeatedly demonstrated her love for her church, town, and its people. While serving as president of the Civic Club, she offered her home for a

Alice Strickland was the first woman mayor in Georgia. She is also credited with starting the first community forest in the state.

clinic, where 20 children had diseased tonsils and adenoids removed. A baby clinic was also held in the Strickland house for the benefit of mothers. Further, she donated a tract of land in the interest of forestry conservation, the first community forest to be started in Georgia, to be planted and used by the children of Duluth for educational and recreational purposes.

Strickland's greatest honor, however, came in 1921 and 1922 when she was elected mayor of Duluth, Georgia, the first woman to hold that position in the state. She was a fearless and forceful mayor, but always attempted to be fair. Applying her business experience to the mayor's office, the astute administrator could not be hoodwinked in the execution of her duties.

Strickland exhibited the same fighting pioneer spirit as her forbears when a power line was to be run across her property in Duluth against her will. Defiantly sitting with a shotgun across her knee, she held up scheduled post hole digging until dinner time, when she had to seek reinforcement—her daughter—to take her place in the name of domestic progress.

Strickland has been recognized posthumously by having a historical marker placed in the yard of her Duluth home in 1999 and by her induction into Georgia Women of Achievement in 2002.

Another native Forsyth Countian who "made good" was John Harold Hawkins, a prominent jurist and civic leader. The son of Perry and Della Bramblett Hawkins, Harold Hawkins was born on May 22, 1892 and, in a few short years, migrated with his family to Marietta where he attended public school. On December 26, 1916, Hawkins was admitted to the bar. He served as official court reporter of the Blue Ridge Circuit from January 1, 1915 to September 1, 1917, and was secretary of the Court of Appeals from September 10, 1917 to March 1, 1920. Subsequently, he practiced law in Marietta from 1920 to 1931 as a member of the firm Morris, Hawkins, and Wallace.

Hawkins's career on the bench began in 1931 as judge of the Blue Ridge Circuit, a position he held from March 1, 1931 to November 30, 1948. Indeed, he was elected four times without opposition. Then, in 1948, when Georgia Chief Justice W.F. Jenkins opted for retirement, Judge Hawkins offered as a candidate for the court vacancy. Elected for a six-year term as Associate Justice, he won reelection without opposition in 1954. Statistics indicate that during his 12 years of service on the Georgia Supreme Court, Hawkins heard 700 cases and prepared 541 written opinions.

Harold Hawkins was a native of Forsyth County who served in the state's judicial system.

Not only did Hawkins serve in the judiciary, but he assumed numerous duties as a civic and social leader in Marietta as well. From 1933 to 1947, he was a member and president of the Board of Education for the city of Marietta; in 1954, he retired after 27 years as Sunday School Superintendent of Marietta First Baptist Church, where he was also a deacon.

The next eight men—a group of heroes who fought for freedom—lost their lives in the service in World War I. The first, Private Ernest Bannister, born on January 23, 1893, entered the service at Camp Gordon in Atlanta in April 1918 and embarked for overseas duty as an attachment of Company M, 327th Infantry, 82nd Division. Bannister was killed in France and his body was returned to Forsyth County almost three years later to be buried at Concord Baptist Church in 1921.

At age 24, Private Benjamin Grady Corn, a Forsyth County farmer, entered the service in December 1917. His service lasted scarcely a month, for he passed away from disease (measles complicated by pneumonia) while attached to Headquarters Company, 307th Engineers, at Camp Gordon. His death came on January 28, 1918 at the Camp Base Hospital. Corn, born on April 29, 1893, was laid to rest in Concord Baptist Church cemetery in the plot with A. Luther and S. Caroline Corn.

Private Dinsmore, a 23-year-old farmer at the time of his induction, was attached to Company C, 350th Infantry subsequent to his basic training. While on duty in France, he contracted pneumonia and passed away on September 29, 1918. His body was returned to Forsyth County almost two years later, and *The Forsyth County News's* August 27, 1920 edition covered the story:

> The body of Mr. Herman Dinsmore, who was killed in France some months ago, was brought to his father's home this week and laid gently to rest at Midway, after funeral services conducted by Rev. R.A. Roper. While we regret the death of this young man, who sacrificed his life for his country, we rejoice in the fact that his body is laid beneath the shade of the trees around his old home where his parents and loved ones can meet and strew flowers of love and friendship o'er his last resting place.

Cemetery records of Midway Methodist Church indicate that Pvt. Dinsmore was born on March 6, 1894.

Private Bryant Ernest Nuckolls, a Forsyth County farmer, entered service from Flowery Branch, Georgia on September 18, 1917 at the age of 21. Following basic training, he was attached to Company B, 102nd Infantry, American Expeditionary Forces. With this unit, he departed for overseas service on June 18, 1918. Nuckolls died in the front line trenches in France on September 26, 1918 and was buried in a cemetery in France, but the graveyard of France did not forever hold the body of Private Nuckolls, for he was returned to the soil of Forsyth County in April 1922. As reported by the *Forsyth County News* on April 22, 1922: "The body . . . arrived at his father's home last Saturday and was laid to rest at Bethel Sunday, with military honors, the funeral services being conducted by Revs. Thompson and Shore."

Drafted from Lawrenceville, Forsyth Countian James Presley Samples entered the service at Camp Gordon on May 29, 1918 and was later transferred to Camp Merritt, New Jersey. He was attached to Company D, 39th Infantry, 4th Division when he embarked for overseas on August 14, 1918. Wounded in action on the Argonne-Meuse front, Corporal Samples died in Evacuation Hospital Number 8 on October 13, 1918. The *Forsyth County News* covered the return of Sample's body in its edition of August 4, 1921: "The body of James Presley Samples arrived last Thursday and was laid away at Corinth. A very large crowd attended the services." In Corinth cemetery, Corporal James Presley Samples's marker reads: "Son of H.D. and L.J.; Corp. Co. D 39 Inf. A.E.F.; born December 28, 1895, died October 13, 1918."

A farmer, age 21, when he received the call to serve, Private Samuel Milton Smith began service on May 29, 1918. He embarked for overseas with the 4th Replacement Detachment and, in France, was transferred to the 60th Machine Gun Company, United States Infantry. While in France, Smith wrote to his mother that he anticipated being home by spring, but he was mistaken, for he was wounded in action at Cunel, France and died from his injuries in Evacuation Hospital Number 22. The body of Private Smith was returned to his native county in the summer of 1921. The *Forsyth County News*, on August 4, 1921, reported: "The body of Sam Smith, who was killed in France, was buried at Concord last Friday. A very large crowd was there to witness the burial, which was a military funeral." Smith's marker in Concord Baptist Church cemetery, in addition to his service notation, records that he was born on January 5, 1896 and died October 19, 1918.

Private Thomas Arp Spence, upon entering the service, was stationed at Camp Gordon in Atlanta prior to his time in France. He was attached to the 328th Infantry, Unassigned, Depot Division, when his family received the following letter from France:

> Dear homefolks: How are you all? I am all O.K. and hope you are the same. I guess you all are at work. I am just laying around for today for it is Sunday and all we do is just lay around. I have never felt better in my life than I do now. Old Russ is as big as a mule. He and I are still together. Guess we will stay together and hope to come back home soon. We are all right so you all need not worry about us. You all have a fine dinner Christmas day for me for I'll be there. We have not got any mail yet but guess it got mixed up. I haven't much time to write before dinner. I am sending Orene and Ada some cards. How is Charlie and Back and Hoke? Has Charlie got to going to see the girls yet, ha ha? Well I guess my dogs are as big as old Bell by this time. Us boys sure do have a big time, for I can't hardly write now for they just keep me tickled to death. I'd love to be at home today and ride about some for I am where

I can't ride now. When I get home I want to swing that big turner plow.
It is dinner so I will close. Arp Spence.

Before Spence's letter was published in the local newspaper, he had contracted influenza and died in France on September 26, 1918. His remains were later returned to Forsyth County, where they were laid to rest in Midway Methodist Church cemetery. His tombstone is simple: "Born March 17, 1896, died September 9, 1918, died in France."

A native Forsyth Countian, Private Jimmy Stewart was born on September 9, 1888. The location at which he was drafted into the service is unknown as his military records have been misplaced over the years. However, he is believed by family members to have died in Germany. Stewart was the son of Andrew W. and Martha J. Stewart, who are buried at Pleasant Grove United Methodist Church.

From war heroes to a sports hero, Luke Appling, who hailed from Cumming in his later years, was a figure who bears remembering. Baseball history buffs are mindful of the personality and style Appling interjected into the game. But what

These were soldiers from Forsyth County who lost their lives in World War I, including Private Ernest D. Bannister, Private Samuel M. Smith, Corporal James Pressly Samples, Private Bryant Ernest Nuckolls, Private Benjamin Grady Corn, Private Herman Dinsmore, and Thomas A. Spence.

Luke Appling, baseball great of yesteryear, spent his last years in Forsyth County. He had retired from the Chicago White Sox in 1950.

was the background of this Hall of Famer? The son of Lucius Appling Sr. and Dola Sappenfield Appling, Lucius Benjamin "Luke" Appling Jr. was born on April 2, 1907 in High Point, North Carolina. Four years later, the Applings moved to Atlanta, where young Luke attended public school and then Oglethorpe University.

In 1930, Luke Appling signed on with the Atlanta Crackers for $1,000. Then, a few short months later, he moved on to the Chicago White Sox at $30,000 and a career that spanned 20 years. During that 20 years, the famous shortstop twice garnered the American League batting title—in 1936 with a .388 average and again in 1943 with .328. When Appling retired in 1950, his career average was an enviable .310, outstanding for a player who approached the game with a host of maladies.

Luke Appling's philosophy of contributing to his team's success was simple. Rather than give in to the physical aches and pains he suffered—indigestion, stiff neck, fallen arches, sore throat, dizzy spells, and insomnia, only to name a few—Appling took out his discomfort on opposing pitchers for 2,749 hits.

Following his retirement from baseball in 1950, Appling was elected to the Hall of Fame in 1964. Then, in 1970, he was accorded another honor when the Chicago Chapter of the Baseball Writers Association of America declared him the greatest player in White Sox history. After retirement, Appling was a roving instructor for the Atlanta Braves from 1972 to 1985.

At the age of 83, Luke Appling passed away on Thursday, January 3, 1991 of an aneurysm at Lakeside Community Hospital in Cumming. Funeral services were held the following Saturday at the Cumming United Methodist Church with burial in Sawnee View Memorial Gardens, Forsyth County.

Returning to women's accomplishments, Alma Kirby Fowler was the second female native of Forsyth County to be credited with a "first." Born in Cumming in 1888, the daughter of John Edward Kirby and Evie Willingham Kirby embarked on a career at the age of 13. Having attended the Hightower Baptist Institute in Cumming, Alma Kirby began working on her father's newspaper, *The North Georgian*. "Miss Alma," as she was known, set the movable type by hand and likewise rolled the press until a kerosene engine was later purchased. Her experience in business and journalism paved the way for an outstanding accomplishment and a "first" in her field. Kirby became owner and editor of her own newspaper, *The Buford Journal*, at the age of just 18. Moreover, Kirby believed that she was the first woman to vote in Forsyth County after the franchise was given to women. Business aside, Alma Kirby married Jarrett Poole Fowler on July 19, 1914.

From farm boy to General Motors executive is the "country boy makes it big" story of Earl Ralph Bramblett. Born on April 14, 1911 in Forsyth County, Earl Ralph Bramblett spent his early boyhood on a farm in the western section of the county near the settlement of Cuba. Then, in about 1920, his father sold the family farm and the John R. Brambletts moved to Smyrna, Georgia, where Earl attended school. Another transition was to follow, for when Earl Bramblett visited his brother Mack, who was employed by General Motors in Flint, Michigan, he likewise decided to join the ranks of the automobile manufacturer—on the assembly line—in Michigan in 1928, a fairly common lifestyle change. However, so remarkable was his next move that it rendered his elevation to the executive level a story extraordinaire. And the skill required? A solid game of golf.

Having been employed on the General Motors assembly line for eight years, Bramblett per chance met Louis Seaton, personnel chief, during a golf game, which became Bramblett's link to the personnel service section of the company. Not only did Bramblett's golf skills impress Seaton, but his management and negotiating abilities came to the fore as well. From the personnel office, Bramblett ascended the corporate ladder with amazing speed. In 1941, he became chief of personnel and, by 1944, he had been transferred to labor relations, a position in which he adroitly represented the company in labor disputes for more than two decades. Indeed, beginning in 1947, he became principal negotiator between General Motors and the United Auto Workers and other unions. In 1970, he succeeded Louis Seaton as head of personnel and chief negotiator, only to be confronted by the company's worst labor problems in 25 years. An astute bargainer, Bramblett led General Motors in settling an eight-week workers' strike by granting employees a 20 percent salary increase on a three-year contract. The company, recognizing the skills and dedication Bramblett had applied in his positions with General Motors, advanced this capable individual to vice president in 1968. Bramblett served in that executive slot until his retirement on October 31, 1971 after a career that spanned 43 years.

Though not a native Forsyth Countian, Ches McCartney, or "Goat Man" as he was known throughout the south, was unusual enough to bear mentioning, for his travels through the county always drew a crowd and captured the imagination of all who viewed his procession. In the 1930s, McCartney had left his job with the WPA near his home in Sigourney, Iowa and decided to try his luck as an itinerant selling postcards. And what an itinerant he proved to be! With a covered wagon constructed of goat skins and a team of 11 or so billies and nannies, Goat Man traversed the country, transporting a load of utilitarian "junk," including wire and leather goat harnesses; wagons of leather, canvas, and goat skins; and pots, pans, a hatchet, lamps, and miscellaneous items. In the 1940s and beyond, onlookers could identify Goat Man by his shoulder-length hair, full beard "to match his goats," goatskin hat, and goatskin clothes. McCartney passed away in 1998 at the approximate age of 97, after spending several years in a nursing home in Jefferson, Georgia.

Back to heroes, the soldiers from Forsyth County who fought in World War II and whose courage and achievements in the face of adversity are too numerous to recount. Nonetheless, some of their war experiences are too poignant to be lost to history. Moreover, memories of the locales where they were based present a positive outlook on the world as they viewed it.

William D. Ferguson had just such recollections of Hawaii prior to the attack of Pearl Harbor.

> I would be remiss if I did not describe Oahu as I first saw it, when I made my first trip around the island in September, 1941. I went to Honolulu and saw Diamond Head from the Waikiki Beach. Of course Waikiki is quite a distance on past Honolulu, but that's where I wound up was Waikiki Beach. I went from there up to Coco Head, which is a big rock on the south side of the island. You could look back and see all Honolulu. Farther around the island, I came into what we called the blowhole. The name of the thing is Kalo Blowhole, or Kalona—I don't know which one it is. It's something like that. Perhaps I had better explain what the blowhole is. There is a cavern under the rocks at the shore where the waves come in. The water fills up the cavern and shoots out through the blowhole. The blowhole is three or four feet across and the water shoots up sometimes as high as fifty feet.

The islands did not remain just interesting places for Ferguson to visit for long.

> Sunday morning, December 7, I had just finished breakfast and came out of the mess hall and picked up an apple which was always laying at

the door on a table. When we stepped into the company street, we saw a lot of planes coming in over Koli Koli Pass. We were to start defense maneuvers the next week and our first thought was that the Air Force was getting ahead of us and starting back. And about that time, Beck Cornears, one of our soldiers, saw the planes and identified them as Japanese. Some of the planes strayed over Wheeler Field; the remainder of the planes flown to and bombed Pearl Harbor and the surrounding areas. They sank the Arizona as well as a number of destroyers, battleships, and destroyed all aircraft that was on the ground. Some planes came in from the north side of the island and hit Kaneohe, Bellas Airfield, and destroyed 99 per cent of all American planes. One of the planes made a dive toward the water tower, which is at upper Schofield Barracks, dropped his bomb, missed the water tower completely. The plane turned and started coming toward the company street. All of us dove under the company barracks. All the mess halls were in line and about the same number of men were coming out of each mess hall. No one was hit. Did I swallow that apple I picked up, or did I drop it? I'll never know.

Another young man, Hoyt Burruss, was reluctant to speak of his war experiences. Years after the war, however, he related that he visited some of the graveyards of

Ches McCartney, known as "Goat Man," was a legend in the south. His treks through Forsyth County never failed to draw a crowd.

Europe and recollected war burial procedure: the dead were placed in sheets and buried with their dog tags in their mouths; a second dog tag was draped over a cross above each grave; when the bodies were removed to be returned home, the two dog tags for each person were expected to match.

Garland Bagley's career as a civilian, converse to the usual military procedure, influenced his service in the army. Having been the principal at Chestatee School for a number of years prior to entering the service, Bagley was skilled in operating a movie projector. When he was stationed in Alabama, he spotted a notice for someone to operate a projector at the camp, applied for the job, and was immediately placed in the operator's position. Shortly before the war ended, Bagley was transferred to North Carolina. Subsequent to his discharge from the army, he set up the Audio-Visual Department for the state of Georgia.

Grady Eugene Wallace remembers being camped by a river in Belgium when some of the soldiers discovered a basement full of cognac and brought back a truck load. Everyone was nipping when one red-headed soldier from Missouri passed out. Inebriated and not in possession of sound judgment at the time, some of the men threw the soldier into the river to revive him. They were afraid he had drowned, but, fortunately, he did survive the experience, although it was necessary for his stomach to be pumped.

In the China-Burma-India Theater of War, Corporal Roy Ernest Wallis recalled when he was in Bombay, India:

> While stationed there . . . I got to visit around some . . . and do some sight-seeing. I visited the Taj Mahal, which is one of the most beautiful buildings there. It is made out of white marble and built between 1632 and 1653 by about 20,000 men. I have a few post card pictures and some snapshots of it. You have to remove your shoes before entering. Shah Jahan and his wife, Mumtazi Mahal, are buried in a tomb there.

The last person inducted into the service from Forsyth County, on April 10, 1946, was C.W. Cox Jr. He served as a "truck driver heavy 931" during his tour of duty in Manila in the Philippines. He was qualified as an M1 Rifle Marksman on May 16, 1946 and later received the World War II Victory Medal. Cox was discharged from the military on April 24, 1947 from the Separation Center at Camp Beale, California.

6. MURDERS

Few events have captured the attention of the citizenry as have murders, particularly those deaths that have resulted from sensational circumstances. The student of history could conclude that Forsyth County has experienced but a minimum of such events throughout the decades.

Sensationalism aside, one may question just what effect these murders have had on the families of the victims, the families of the perpetrators, and, indeed, even the perpetrators themselves. The Claiborn Vaughan murder, from this perspective, is an example of the senselessness of some murders and their widespread aftermath.

The day began normally enough. Saturday, August 7, 1858 was Justice of the Peace court day in the Wildcat community. Residents of the area gathered, as they usually did, to hear the proceedings, partake of the supplies from the "liquor wagon," and, in general, to socialize with one another.

The Vaughans and Buices were drinking and grumbling with the Freelands and Pettyjohns, who were likewise imbibing liberally. The group finally moved to a different location, about a half-mile away, where they engaged in a shooting match. Then, a disagreement ensued as to who was the winner of the match.

This particular argument was continued back at the courthouse, where the hostile groups again drank and continued to flare at one another. At some point, the Freelands and Pettyjohns referred to the Vaughans and Buices as thieves and forgers who had been ousted from South Carolina.

At about 9 p.m., the Vaughans and Buices headed home with the Freelands and Pettyjohns following. Being wary of potential danger, some of the Vaughans and Buices hid out and waited for the rival faction to pass them. Claiborn Vaughan, however, continued on the road. His body would be found later on this same road—Hemrick Road or Clement Road, as it was known—about a mile from Big Creek School.

Subsequently, on Sunday and into Monday, a coroner's inquest was held and several individuals from the area, who were involved or were witnesses to the "bad blood" between the two groups, testified then and later before a grand jury. The outcome of the grand jury proceedings was that Isaac Freeland was indicted for murder as principal in the first degree, while Jacob Pettyjohn, Levi McGinnis,

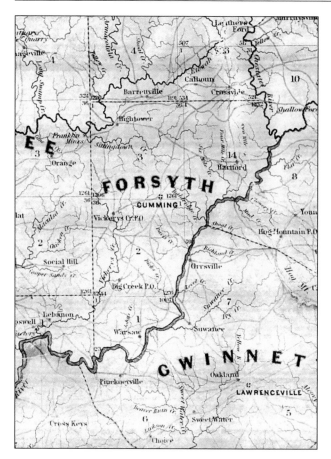

The Isaac Freeland murder was committed at Big Creek, also called Wildcat. Big Creek was located several miles southwest of Cumming, the seat of Forsyth County.

William Brannon, and James McGinnis were likewise indicted for murder, but in the second degree. The grand jury record from the August 1858 term of Superior Court indicates that all the accused "feloniously, willfully, unlawfully and of their malice aforethought did kill and murder."

Isaac Freeland was tried first, in February 1859, and convicted on circumstantial evidence. The inquest had determined that Vaughan had died from deep knife wounds, one of which had severed his left jugular vein. Not only had Freeland been found with blood on his clothing, but he had returned to the scene to attempt to locate his missing knife. Following his conviction, Freeland was hanged on April 15, 1859—the first hanging to be carried out in Forsyth County.

Jacob Pettyjohn's fate was entirely different. Like Freeland, he was tried and convicted. Although he was sentenced to hang on June 24, 1859, his lawyer H.P. Bell was successful in seeking a new trial. Pettyjohn was taking no chances, however. He managed to escape and run for Texas, where he was never apprehended.

The trial of Levi McGinnis was predictable. He was convicted and sentenced to hang. The notes of Garland Bagley indicate that McGinnis, too, escaped, but was captured in Corinth, Mississippi. At any rate, he was also granted a new trial, but the Georgia Supreme Court upheld the lower court's conviction and ordered a private hanging. Thus, McGinnis was hanged in the jail in Cumming on March 15, 1861. He and Freeland were both buried in unmarked graves in the Piney Grove/Bagley cemetery.

William Brannon and James McGinnis were tried jointly. Both were found guilty and served three years in the penitentiary.

One can imagine the anguish, bitterness, and prolonged suffering of the families involved—both those of the victim and of the perpetrators. But how long would the pain extend? A letter from the great-great-granddaughter of Isaac Freeland averred that knowledge of the hanging of her ancestor had precipitated strong emotions among his descendants more than 140 years after the tragedy:

> It still seems like some kind of dream. You see, neither I nor any of my relatives knew anything about all this until just a few weeks [ago]. My Forsyth County relatives were as shocked as I was and wouldn't believe me until I showed them absolute proof.
>
> . . . we went to the courthouse and read some of the court record of the trial. We didn't have time to read it all, but I made copies of 50 something pages and brought them home. That night we all met at Uncle Hoyt's house and had a reading and discussing session. Isaac Freeland was my great-great-grandfather and Howell E. Freeland my great-grandfather. We are sure Great-grandpa Howell E. never told my grandpa anything about the hanging. I used to ask Grandpa a lot of questions about the "old times," and he knew very little about his father's people—not even his grandfather's name or any of his aunts and uncles on the Freeland side. He thought his father came from "somewhere up north."
>
> All of Isaac's children left Forsyth County, near as I can learn, after the hanging. My great-grandfather raised his family in one of the most remote sections of the North Georgia mountains. He was almost fanatically opposed to the making or drinking of alcohol in any form.
>
> It is such a strange coincidence that my grandfather settled down to live in the very county where his father was born without even knowing it. He was always hearing about some place where the grass might be a little greener and moved around a lot. He finally moved to Cherokee County and then on to Forsyth about 1917, so he could raise cotton . . . . Upon learning that his name was Freeland, someone told him that a Freeland was hung in Cumming a long time ago. He didn't think much about it, because he didn't think he was related to the man.
>
> This summer I have gotten in touch with as many of Isaac's descendants as possible. As far as I can learn, none of Isaac's children (except his youngest daughter who was seven in 1859) ever told any of their children or anybody about their father, Isaac. He has a large number of great-grandchildren scattered over the U.S. They all are

finding the news of Isaac very upsetting. I wanted to learn all I could, but am now wishing I had kept my big mouth shut. They are a generation closer to it than I am and can feel more of what a tragedy it was in the lives of their grandparents.

From all I can learn about Isaac's children from relatives and other sources, they all had much the same qualities. They were quiet, kind and tender-hearted, working hard and minding their own business. They were all deeply religious and truthful and honest to an extreme degree. While none of them would be anybody's door mat, they never started trouble and were good and respectful citizens in their communities. Hardly the kind of children you would expect a murderer to raise!

I wonder if you have run across the story I have heard from two completely independent sources. Uncle Hoyt was doing some carpenter work in the old wildcat area a dozen or more years ago. Some old man asked him if he was related to the Freeman who was hung in Cumming years ago. Uncle Hoyt said that as far as he knew he wasn't related. Then the old man told him the story of the hanging but said that much later another man confessed on his deathbed to helping murder Vaughan and then planting Isaac's knife beside Vaughan . . . and said that Isaac fought with Vaughan but had no part in helping kill him.

Just this summer one of Isaac's great-granddaughters wrote me the same confession story with slight variations and said that she heard it years ago from someone who moved from Forsyth County to the state where she lives.

The man who told Uncle Hoyt the story said that people had wondered why Isaac did not appeal. Some thought that because of the knife used, Isaac might have thought one of his sons did it. There had been trouble before between Freelands and Buices, according to him. I think it is possible that Isaac was too intoxicated to remember very well just what happened that night, and because evidence pointed that way, thought he might have done it whether he did or not.

I guess what I am leading up to is a plea to please be kind to my great-great-grandpa. I can't expect you not to tell the story, since it is a part of history, but it would also be true to history to say that there is a story told of a deathbed confession which says that Isaac was innocent . . . Maybe he did kill Vaughan in the heat of anger or the stupidity of alcohol, but he could have been innocent. There will be a lot of grateful Freelands if you can see your way to tell his story so that those who read it won't think he was too terrible. Maybe he was terrible, but I hope not.

The second murders to be examined occurred later in the century and involved two sisters from Forsyth County who died in Clayton, Georgia.

Beginning in the present, the setting is tranquil: the back ridge of Cumming Cemetery. However, the inscription on the joint grave marker of Ella Beck and

The joint grave marker for Ella Beck and Addie Bailey is found in Cumming Historic Cemetery. The Bailey sisters are buried in close proximity to the grave of their parents, Dr. Samuel S. and Sarah P. Bailey.

Addie Bailey belies the plot's peaceful surroundings. The heart-rending story of the sisters is outlined thusly:

ELLA N. BECK   ADDIE E. BAILEY

AGE *19* YEARS   AGE *17* YEARS

ELLA AND ADDIE WERE MURDERED AT CLAYTON, RABUN COUNTY, ON THE NIGHT OF
OCTOBER *28, 1884,* BY EUGENE W. BECK, ELLA'S INTEMPERATE HUSBAND.
SWEETLY SLEEP, ANGEL SISTERS,
NO MORE FROM YOUR SLUMBER
WILL YOU BE AWAKENED BY PISTOL SHOTS
FROM THE BOTHERS OF EARTH YOU WERE DRIVEN,
BUT THE GATES OF HEAVEN WERE OPENED TO LET YOU IN

Who were these young women whose lives were snuffed out in 1884? In close proximity to the sisters' graves lie those of their parents, Dr. Samuel S. and Sarah P. Bailey. Born on June 26, 1811 in Rutherford County, North Carolina, Dr. Bailey died in Forsyth County on February 17, 1887. His second wife and mother of the slain sisters, Sarah P. Bailey, was the daughter of Lindsey Edwards. Born in Walker County on March 19, 1848, she died on October 5, 1904 in Forsyth County.

As the story of the sisters' deaths unfolded, the *Gainesville Herald* offered the following account of the tragedy:

> Clayton, Georgia, November 1, 1884. On Wednesday I telegraphed you the killing and fatally wounding of Mrs. Beck, of this place, and Miss Addie Bailey of Cumming. Miss Bailey died this afternoon at 5 o'clock. It appears that Mr. Beck had been drinking for the past 29 days, not being sober the whole time up to the night of the killing.
>
> In the evening about 9 o'clock, I heard screams for help and on going out of my room heard two pistol shots in the direction of Mr. Beck's house just across the street. I hurried over there and found both ladies in bed. Mrs. Beck with a wound in her head and a portion of her brain on the outside was lifeless, and Miss Bailey, lying on her side, shot through the chest, calling for someone to finish killing her or to help her. Dr. Smith, being on hand, gave his attention at once to Miss Bailey and sent a dispatch for the father, Dr. Bailey of Cumming, to come at once. Dr. Bailey arrived here Thursday morning to find one daughter a corpse and the other almost dead. Miss Bailey was to have been married next Sunday morning to a man of this place.
>
> Mr. Beck, arraigned before Magistrates Long and Derrick, and after hearing evidence, was found guilty of murder in the first degree and bound over for trial at the March term of court.
>
> Susan Miller, colored, being sworn, said that on the night of the 28th inst., she and Mrs. Beck were at work in Mrs. Beck's sleeping room when Mr. Beck lay down and took a nap of sleep . . . About ten minutes after Miss Addie had retired, Mr. Beck got up and put on his boots. He then jumped on the bed that contained the ladies and, putting one knee on his wife, shot her with a pistol. He then turned and snapped at the witness who was standing out of the room. As she passed through the door, she turned her head and saw him raise the cover with his left hand and shoot Miss Bailey. She was standing at the foot of the bed when he fired the first shot. She then started upstairs to awake the men who were boarding with the Becks, and when she got back Mr. Beck was gone. The witness stated that she never heard any threats made—only when he was under the influence of whiskey, when he would say, "I will shoot directly." There was never any fussing between the husband and wife, and they always seemed good to each other. He shot her with a pistol as the witness saw it. Mrs. Beck died instantly.
>
> William Dillingham, being sworn, testified that on the 28th of October Eugene Beck came to him to borrow a pistol to shoot some dogs that had been prowling around his house at night; that Mr. Beck had borrowed the pistol once before and also a gun from Mr. Duncan to shoot the dogs. Mr. Dillingham loaned the pistol reluctantly. Mr. Beck said he wanted to shoot a dog or a ____ hog. Mr. Dillingham then went

to supper leaving Mr. Beck standing at the door and saw no more of him until after the shooting. Mr. Dillingham was sitting in his room and heard two shots fired. In a few minutes Mr. Beck came into his room saying, "Cap (Captain Dillingham), they run in on me, two of them, and I shot them." Mr. Dillingham then asked Mr. Beck for his pistol. Mr. Beck gave it to him saying that he surrendered and to let no one hurt him. Mr. Dillingham, telling Mr. Beck to sit down, ran out to see what was the matter and what was meant by the hollering. He found that Mr. Beck had killed his wife. He then returned to his room where he had left Mr. Beck and told him that he had killed his wife. Mr. Beck said that if he had done so, then he had killed the best friend he had. "There were two barrels of the pistol empty and another had been snapped without firing." Dr. Smith testified to the character of the wounds. Mr. Beck was bound over for trial at the next term of court.

Your correspondent visited Mr. Beck in jail this evening and found him quite willing to talk. I asked him how he was feeling. He replied that he was feeling some better than he had been. I then asked him how come him to shoot his wife and sister-in-law. He says that he deplores the act and while he trusts that God would forgive him, he knew the law would not and he wanted to be hanged for his crime. He stated that he and his wife had always lived peaceable and happily together, and in her death he had lost his best friend and true wife. Mr. Beck further stated that if the doors of the jail were thrown open, he would not leave; he would rather die than live.

The senseless murder of sisters Addie Bailey and Ella Beck in Clayton, Georgia on October 28, 1884 elicited two letters from a half-sister of the victims, Minnie Bailey Julian, to the perpetrator, Eugene W. Beck, husband of Ella. Excerpts are printed here:

Who welcomed me upon your threshold? My (once our) father, bowed with age and grief, and a vast throng of weeping friends, as I entered the door of your dim lighted dwelling, supported by father and husband, who greeted me with pleasant smile and warm kisses. Ah, what do I see? A coffin containing the cold, lifeless form of my once bright-eyed, merry sister, Ella, your wife. I knelt, clasped the box, and poured out my grief to God; 'twas all that I could do, for the murdered, mangled, sweet face was nailed and sealed from view.

My father said, "Arise, my daughter, and go further on." I pressed through the dining room, thence to your room. There upon your bed was laid the lifeless form of sister Addie. The warm life-blood that you had drawn had paled the cheek, but the pleasant smile lingered there as if but asleep. Around the death couch stood your friends and hers, dressing her in the robes that were to have been her bridal costume.

There I knelt again and kissed the cold lips and marble brow and thought of you. How? As a murderer? No, no, I could, I would not. I arose and seated myself by your dismal hearthstone.

The funeral was equally as grim. The bodies of Ella Beck and Addie Bailey were brought back to Cumming via the train from Clayton to Buford and then on to Cumming by wagon. Upon the arrival of the family and corpses in Cumming, the following scene ensued, as described by Minnie Julian:

One more heart-rending meeting—that of the bereaved lover [J.A. Swafford] with the mother of his dead bride and other relatives. He thought he was strong and wanted to meet with and mourn with those dear to "his Addie." But it was too much for his youth. Fainting, he would have fallen had they not borne him to the couch. I was standing a little aside.

My step-mother said, "Oh, Sis, go . . . to . . . "

She was carried from the room unconscious. The long night watch followed.

Minnie Bailey Julian, who wrote poignantly of the double murder, was a half-sister to Ella Beck and Addie Bailey.

Eugene W. Beck, it must be related, died in the Rabun County jail before his death sentence could be carried out—of lead poisoning that had built up in his body as a result of the whiskey he had been drinking.

The next murder of note, that of Dewitt "Gilly" Thomas in 1941, was likewise alcohol-related. And, like the Bailey/Beck sisters, the victim was buried in Cumming Cemetery. In fact, the cemetery was the scene of his murder as well.

The discovery of Gilly Thomas's body on Sunday, June 29, 1941, spurred an investigation that culminated in the trial of Josiah Phillips at the August term of court in 1941. With the Honorable Clifford Pratt presiding, the State, lead by Solicitor General H.G. Vandiviere and Phil Landrum, and the defendant's attorneys, Wood, Spence, and Garland Brown, paraded a series of witnesses through the courtroom with varying accounts of the events prior to and subsequent to the death of Thomas in Case #1848, *The State* v. *Josiah Phillips*.

First to testify was Dr. Marcus Mashburn, who was called to examine the body on the morning of June 29 along with a Coroner's Jury. Dr. Mashburn asserted that the body was clothed in a shirt, underwear, shoes, and socks. He noted that the shoes had no mud on them. The cause of death? The conclusion was injuries plus dirt. Specifically, concussion of the brain, shock from the concussion, exposure, and dirt in the mouth and nose that could have interfered with breathing.

Next, funeral director Royston Ingram, who removed the body from Cumming Cemetery, gave an account of the murder scene: the body of Thomas was lying near the grave of Mr. and Mrs. Ed Puett in the northeast corner of the cemetery; the head was southwest of the feet; near the corpse was a bloody marble slab, approximately 10 inches square and one-half-inch thick. There were severe cuts on the bridge of the nose and 1.25 inches under the left eye. The mouth and left nostril were filled with dirt, mixed with saliva and packed to some extent. Based on rigor mortis and discoloration, Thomas had likely been deceased for 12 to 14 hours when the examination took place.

Establishing the events leading up to the murder and those that ensued tended to be a tedious process as the numerous witnesses told their versions of the scenario. On Saturday night, June 28, 1941, citizens and former citizens were converging on the town of Cumming in anticipation of the June Singing the following day. Alton Porter, who worked in Atlanta, had arrived by bus at approximately 6 p.m. and disembarked in front of the Poole and Orr Cafe. He then met up with Joel Webb, Gilly Thomas, and Joe Phillips at John Black's service station. Another key player in the evening's activities, Otis Hurt, who was Gilly Thomas's brother-in-law, asserted that he arrived between 5:00 and 6:00, saw Gilly Thomas out in front of the new post office, Webb in the drug store about 9 p.m., and never saw Josiah Phillips at all. Interestingly, Hurt employed attorney Lyles to sit in on the trial.

Joel Webb testified that he arrived from Atlanta on Friday, saw Gilly Thomas and Josiah Phillips at the Five Points service station on Saturday, and went with them and Alton Porter in O.C. Wilburn's car to Ab Glover's, who illegally sold alcohol, to buy liquor for the four. On the trip back to Cumming, the group stopped at Pendley's and bought a chaser, then returned to the Five Points station, where he left with George McClure and his brother. Thomas and Phillips had left the station headed down the highway.

Just who went with whom to Ab Glover's, and when, was the focus of the trial for a time. Alton Porter declared that he went with a "Green boy" in a 1940 V-8—along with Webb, Thomas, and Phillips—to Glover's for about an hour. They stopped at Clyde Pendley's on the way back to take a drink and, while they were there, an argument started between he and Webb. Back at the Five Points station, proprietor Ed Fowler ran them off because of their inebriated condition. A disagreement had arisen at the station when a man named Majors wanted Thomas to play poker, but he had consumed too much alcohol to be an effective player. Gilly Thomas had then suggested going back to Glover's.

If establishing the liquor connection and its ramifications was an integral part of the case for both the prosecution and defense, the inconsistencies in the stories of the witnesses cast as many doubts over the testimony as they clarified—perhaps more so. How many trips were made to Ab Glover's for liquor? Who was in the car each time? Did arguments break out that may have led to murder?

Bud Hamby, a man who resided in the Italy community, testified that he was at Ab Glover's when Phillips, Thomas, Porter, and others were standing around a "new-looking" car and talking with women who were apparently with them. Then Mrs. W.W. Goss, a resident who lived south of Cumming, told of two women—Gladys Fields and daughter Bettie Brannon—coming to her house at about 2 a.m. in a car with a man wearing shades. At about 9 a.m. the next morning, the two women left a suitcase at her house and departed for the June Singing. The part, if any, played by the women and their knowledge of the murder was never determined, for Sheriff Ira Sewell claimed he could not find them after Sunday to serve a subpoena.

At any rate, liquor was purchased and the boisterous behavior of the revelers was observed by certain townsfolk. Alton Porter and Granville Majors argued at Five Points station and Ed Fowler called the marshall. Subsequently, witnesses saw Thomas and Phillips making their way toward Cumming Cemetery, "helping each other," although not always successfully, to stay on their feet. Another witness, Roscoe Spears, testified that, while in jail, Phillips told him that a car drove up and stopped at the cemetery. Phillips, Webb, Thomas, and Porter got out. The row that had begun at Fowler's was renewed at the cemetery. Porter knocked Thomas out and all three carried him up into the cemetery, where Phillips must have hit him with a piece of marble. Phillips said he then went and sat down in the weeds. The next morning, Thomas's body would be discovered in the cemetery. Later, Phillips averred he did not know why he was wearing Thomas's clothing, but he knew where his own had been left.

Josiah Phillips did not remain in the cemetery that night, but made his way to Buford. After being too drunk to remember anything, Phillips maintained he was dumped from a car in the Haw Creek community. Doyle Gilbert, who lived in Alabama and was visiting his sister Stella Sizemore, picked up Phillips around midnight near the junction of the old and new roads near Haw Creek and took him to the ice plant in Buford. According to Gilbert, he did not want to risk being caught with no taillights and, thus, did not drive into the main part of town. At the ice plant, the proprietor noticed that Phillips was clad in a green suit and army shirt and had blood on his hands. Phillips purportedly related to him that he had been drinking "pop-skull" liquor, had had a fight with Gilly Thomas, and had left Thomas in bad shape.

From the ice plant, an intoxicated Phillips proceeded on foot to the main business district, where patrolman Earl Sears remembered seeing him in the middle of the street and later in a restaurant associated with a taxi cab business. Chief Murphy of Buford was also in the restaurant and relieved Phillips of his liquor when Phillips attempted to take a drink in the establishment. The cook on duty at the restaurant, Edward Myers, remembered Phillips going to the back of the business and washing his hands, after which the water "looked red, like blood." Shortly thereafter, patrolman Sears took Phillips to jail because he had been drinking. At that time, Phillips gave his name as "Anderson."

The story, confusing enough up to this point, was further muddied by Otis Hurt, who claimed when talking with Buford Police Chief Murphy on Sunday, June 29

Dewitt "Gilly" Thomas was found murdered in Cumming Cemetery. His body was discovered on June 29, 1941, the day citizens were convening on the town of Cumming for the annual June Singing.

The Forsyth County Courthouse, completed in 1905, served until 1973 when it was burned by arsonists.

that he had pointed out Phillips to Sheriff Ira Sewell on produce row in Atlanta. Hurt had come home to Buford, purchased a shirt and hat at Bass's Store, and proceeded to Buford Jail. He then wandered inside the jail with a sack in his hand, stayed about five minutes, and left. Hurt, it must be noted, had spent early Sunday morning dodging Chief Pharr in Cumming by making his way near the cemetery.

Then there was the question of the clothes. Why was Josiah Phillips wearing the dead man's clothing after the murder? And why was Phillips's army uniform discovered across the highway and somewhat south of the cemetery? Was Phillips framed for the murder? At last, the State rested and Josiah Phillips was able to make the following lengthy statement:

> Gentlemen, on the fourth Saturday in June, I met Gilly Thomas down here at Mr. Brooks' Store. He was talking to Ralph Holbrooks. Gilly came up and shook hands with me and asked me how I was getting along. Then he asked me did I want a drink of whiskey, and I says "Yes,

I don't care." We went over to Mr. George Morris' warehouse and drank half a pint of M & M red whiskey, which he had brought from Atlanta with him. Then we went over to the Five Points Service Station and met up there with Alton Porter and Joel Webb. Mr. Porter had nearly a half pint of white whiskey. Well, we four drank it. Then Alton says we want some more whiskey and we was all willing to go and get it.

This boy—I can't call his name—works for the Otwell Motor Company, drove up and stopped. Alton went out and asked him would he carry us for the [price of] gasoline. Joel Webb said he would buy the gasoline. He said he would carry us for the gasoline. We stopped at the Buford cross roads filling station, bought three gallons of gasoline, which he, Webb, paid for. We went on down to Mr. Ab Glover's.

We drove up in the driveway. We didn't get out, any of us except Porter. Ab came out and asked us how much did we want. Gilly first told him a quart, and Alton says a pint will be enough. Gilly Thomas bought the whiskey and paid for it. Then, gentlemen, we turned around there and didn't make another stop until we got to Mr. Clyde Pendley's filling station.

We pulled up kinder to the right of his filling station, kinder behind the station, and bought a chaser and went to drinking. Gentlemen, there was a little fight. Alton slapped him with his hand. Gilly was calling him a [derogatory name]. And put him in the back of the automobile. Mr. Egbert Payne came out near the car and told us we would have to leave or quieten down. We left.

Then we came back to headquarters, the Five Points Filling Station. We got out and went in and still drank some more whiskey. Alton Porter he had some few words with a fellow named Majors. Him and Gilly also had some words, too. Gilly was getting pretty drunk, but he could walk all right, and Gilly wanted to go and gamble, but Porter wouldn't let him.

Then Gilly and Porter and Webb and myself wanted to go back and get some more whiskey. Porter says I know a fellow out in town that will carry us. We will go get him and be back in a few minutes. Before they came back, Mr. Ed Fowler, that run the place, had sent the little Majors boy after the Chief of Police. Gilly was cursing and raising sand with all the customers that came around. Before Alton Porter and Joel Webb got back, Fowler asked me would I carry him out behind the filling station. He says "I will check up and get out and help you; if you don't, the police will take him down."

Well he was hollering and cursing back behind the filling station. I knew if the police came, he would get him there. So we walked down the road. We never did cross that dirt road, gentlemen. Which Gilly, he was very drunk, but he could walk.

Alton Porter, Joel Webb and Otis Hurt, Mrs. Hendrix and her daughter came along in a Ford V-8. Hurt said it was George McClure's car—I don't know whose it was—and picked us up. So we went down to Ab's.

We drove on the left side of the road next to the old filling station and stopped the car and he said we wouldn't get no whiskey if we all went over to the house, that he would go by himself and get the whiskey and we could stay with the automobile. Otis Hurt, Gilly Thomas and myself got out of the automobile but stayed close around. He was gone about ten minutes. Alton Porter was gone about ten minutes and brought the whiskey, bought one pint, was all we had.

Then we turned around there and drove back up the highway and didn't make a stop until we got out here to what you call the King farm. They was fighting a little all along. We got out there. Porter and Gilly, they had a fight. A few licks passed between them. Otis Hurt, he smacked Gilly a few times but got back in the car. Alton Porter went up to Otis and said something I didn't hear, and he went on. Left Alton Porter, Gilly Thomas, Joel Webb and myself standing there at the old deserted filling station. We came on out the road then to the graveyard.

Right at the far end from here, right next to the high part of it, the fight got started again. Porter, he hit several licks with a black jack and knocked him in a little ditch about a foot and a half deep. I was the only friend that Gilly Thomas had out there. I pulled him out of the ditch and taken my handkerchief from my pocket and wiped his mouth off and nose, which was bleeding pretty fast. Otis Hurt . . . First, though, Alton Porter saw the lights of a car coming over the hill at Mr. A.J. Fowler's. He says "Let's carry Gilly up in the graveyard there," which Gilly was hurt.

We picked Gilly up. I put my left arm around his neck. Porter was next to me helping to carry his body up. Joel Webb was carrying his legs. We carried him up in the graveyard by that tree by the house, back of the path, about ten feet from the road. Laid him down. Gilly was lying on his back. Otis Hurt, he pulls up a little ways, up about the dirt road, and stopped and gets out and comes up. Alton Porter and I washed the blood off of his mouth and nose again. I got down on my knees; my handkerchief was wet with blood, and the last time I taken Gilly's shirt tail and wiped the blood off of his face with his own shirt tail. I told Porter to get up and look at these gashes on his face you done made with the black jack. Porter got up and turned him over so that he kindly was setting up straight on the ground. I looked at him and Gilly kept getting up on his left shoulder. And Porter goes back with the little tombstone and hits him in the face with it, three or four licks, and Gilly fell backwards and stretched out and threw his arms over.

I told Porter I wouldn't do a dog that way. So he says if you don't hush you will get the same thing. He was talking on loud. You could have heard him for thirty or forty steps. Otis Hurt says you had better put your hand over his mouth; someone will hear us. He says "Wait" and he put something in his mouth, I don't know what.

Me and Webb went down in the lower end of the cemetery down next to the fill where you come up at, only we was about ten or fifteen feet from the road, sitting in the weeds. We had taken a drink or two. And Porter came down by himself. Hurt wasn't with him. I had taken a drink or two. He says, "I know Joel Webb won't say anything about this," and he says "You had better not." About all I could say was no. The last I remember there we was all three sitting in the weeds drinking.

The next thing I remember then, gentlemen, was about one mile below Haw Creek Church. I was then pulled out of an automobile and tossed down a fill about three or four feet high, right opposite a mud hole. It kinder jolted me up a little. There was more than one man and some women. I could hear the men talking, but I didn't know them. One of the men says, "Phillips may talk," and he says, "I am going to go down there and stomp his teeth down his throat." And one of the girls spoke up and says, "Otis, Phillips won't talk; don't do it."

And they got in the car and left. It was a '40 V-8. I got up in about ten minutes. I was still jolted up a little bit and was standing by this mud hole. Then this A-Model Ford came out this old Haw Creek Road. I didn't try to stop them. I was standing by this mud hole. I didn't know where I was. I was looking around trying to locate the country. They drove past me into the new road. . . . They stopped. And one of the Pruitt boys got out and says, "Joe, if you want to ride, come on."

I got in the back seat between Pruitt and another fellow I didn't know. I don't know the other two. There was a girl along. I didn't know her. One of the Pruitt boys was in the front seat. We went on down, got almost to the river and I asked them where we was. They said they was on the Buford Highway and that they was riding around for a pastime, and if I wanted to go to Buford I could, but they was a little low in gasoline. I says I haven't got any money much but I will give you a quarter, which I taken out of my shirt pocket.

We were drunk then. The girl was drunk, and we all drank whiskey. I had nearly a half pint that these boys left on me. They had a pint of whiskey and we all was drinking. We didn't make a stop until we got to the ice plant. When we got to the ice plant, they said they wouldn't go on in town because they didn't have a tail light on the automobile. We all got out except the girl and got a Coca Cola. We drank the Coca Colas and whiskey, too. One of the Pruitt boys paid for the Coca Colas. There was a man working with his ice on the inside, but he never did come out, only to get pay for his Coca Colas, and then went back.

There was a big guy that come up I didn't know, on the outside. He asked me my name. I told him, and I told him where I lived. I asked him his, but I don't remember his name. I asked him did he know Theodore Pirkle. He said he did. I told him that we used to go to school together. I told him that some of the boys that night had a fight with one of my best friends and I thought they had hurt him very seriously. But gentlemen, that is all I told him. I asked him then was there a taxi cab place in Buford. He said there was, and I asked him how far it was to Buford. He said about one mile.

I wobbled on out to Buford. I don't remember seeing anybody until I got to this taxi cab place. I went in the restaurant. I ordered a hot dog. I didn't eat this hot dog until I asked the man could I wash my hands. I had blood on my hands that I got off of Gilly Thomas by wiping the blood off of him. And the boy says, "You can wash your hands." I went back and washed my hands and came back and ate the hot dog. I didn't drink any whiskey at that time. Then I pulled out this bottle. There wasn't very much whiskey in this half-pint bottle. I pulled it out and went to take a drink and a police officer walked in at the door and walked over and taken the whiskey from me, walked back to the door and poured it out. I ate the other hot dog.

I got up and walked out in front of the restaurant. I was talking to the taxi driver about bringing me back to Cumming. I asked them what they would charge me. They said two dollars. About that time a police officer came out and asked me did I ___. "Well I will carry you down and lock you up and turn you out in the morning or get you sobered up a little bit and then turn you out in the morning." The next morning if he came down I didn't know it. I was either drunk or asleep. That was on Sunday.

Well on Sunday evening about five o'clock Otis Hurt comes over. He has my soldier uniform with him in a big paper sack like you go to the store and buy a hat. He come in and he says, "Phillips, I got your uniform here, but I can't put it in at the hole at the door." I says take the pants and put them in and then put the shirt in. On the outside, there was four or five standing on the outside. There was a colored man in the jail. He saw this also. He says, "I will tell you what I will do." He says, "I will take your clothes, your uniform, back over to Cumming and I will put them on the side of the road next to a pine tree right above the Cumming springs." I don't know whether he did or not. So he left.

The next morning was Monday morning. The police came down. He says, "What's your name?" I says, "Joe Phillips." He says, "Where do you live." I says "Cumming, Georgia, Forsyth County." He says, "You are in the army." I says 'Yes'. "What company?" "Twenty-second Infantry, Company A." He says, "Do you know Gilly Thomas?" I says, "Yes, he's a good friend of mine." He says, "Did you know he was dead?" I says "No." Otis Hurt told me Gilly Thomas wasn't dead and wasn't hurt much. That's why I didn't know he was dead. The police says, "I will call the sheriff from your county and the State Patrol from Gainesville," and they did. They come and carried me to Canton.

On Monday morning, or either Tuesday morning, the solicitor come up in jail. I told him that I didn't remember anything about the whole business. I was drunk. Why I told him that I didn't have no lawyer and I didn't want to talk about it. I didn't trust him. On Thursday or Friday, I wont befo' sure, he comes back. I told him where he could find the clothes, just what Otis Hurt told me. I don't know where Otis Hurt put the clothes there or not. He said he would, and that is all I told the solicitor. And so far as the deputy sheriff of Cherokee County says what I said, he swore a lie; that isn't true. Gentlemen, Otis Hurt and Alton Porter killed Gilly Thomas. I didn't kill him. I was the only friend that he had out there. And I done all I could for him when the others were killing him; I thank you all.

Josiah Phillips's testimony apparently did not convince the jury of his innocence, for the panel found him—not guilty of murder as charged—but of voluntary manslaughter. On August 30, 1941, he was sentenced to serve five to ten years in prison.

A fourth murder, with Benjamin Perry Roper as the victim, occurred approximately two years after the death of Gilly Thomas in Cumming Cemetery.

Merchant, banker, agribusinessman, Roper, a prominent citizen of the Cuba settlement in the Friendship community of Forsyth County, descended from

Benjamin P. Roper was fatally wounded at his general store at Cuba. Robbery was the motive for his brutal beating.

103

pioneers who migrated into the area prior to 1850. Born on August 4, 1868, Roper married Maggie Tribble, daughter of Newton and Canzada Sams Tribble, in 1894. During his lifetime, "Ben" Roper, as he was known in the community, engaged in numerous business pursuits and other activities. Not only did he operate a general store, but he also ran a cotton gin, owned and officiated as president of the Bank of Cumming, and served as Postmaster of Cuba, Georgia from December 22, 1902 to October 17, 1903, when the post office was discontinued. A member of Friendship Baptist Church, Roper chaired the Building Committee in 1919.

Roper's success as a local merchant may have ultimately led to his death in 1943 from a skull fracture suffered at the hands of robbers at his general store beside his dwelling house. Roper died on February 25, 1943 from injuries sustained in a robbery three days earlier. He left behind wife Maggie and four children.

The scenario had begun to unfold on Friday, February 19, when two individuals identified as Walter Fowler, a Marine, and Austin Watson, a tenant on Roper's property, entered the store of Linton H. Tribble on Canton Highway, ostensibly to purchase Coca-Colas, candy, sweet crackers, and a gallon of kerosene. Later that afternoon, Tribble would discover that his .32 caliber automatic pistol, resembling a German luger, was missing. Though never recovered, the pistol was

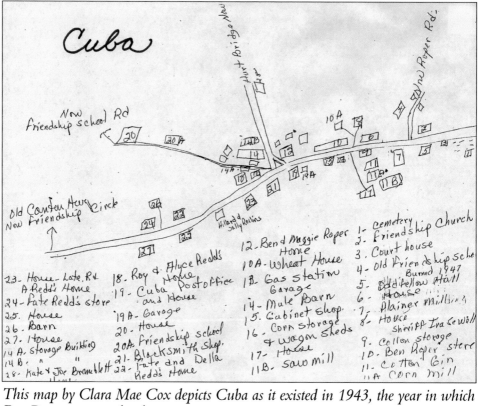

This map by Clara Mae Cox depicts Cuba as it existed in 1943, the year in which Ben Roper was murdered.

believed to be one of the two weapons used to administer the fatal blows to Roper the following Monday.

What events took place that Monday in Ben Roper's Store? It was not until the following day when Roper regained consciousness for about three hours in Georgia Baptist Hospital that the episode would be related—answers anxiously awaited by a stunned family and community. Fortunately, Roper was able to name his attackers.

It is unclear how Roper, after his unmerciful beating, could lock up his store and traverse the short distance from the store building to his home. Yet a salesman, Ben Palmer, discovered Roper in his rocking chair and summoned help. Maggie Roper sped from the back of the house. Palmer and nearby blacksmith Corbett Galloway rushed to Cumming for Sheriff Ira Sewell, while Dr. Rader Hugh Bramblett and Dr. P.W. Tribble attempted to aid the fatally injured victim until an ambulance could arrive to transport him to Georgia Baptist Hospital in Atlanta.

On February 23, the day after Roper's attack, a search of the nearby area was conducted. Two sets of tracks leading from an old field road behind Friendship Church toward Friendship School were discovered. A short distance into the woods, a limb that had been moved was noted. Upon turning the limb over, the searchers beheld a green shirt and a pair of overalls containing cigarettes. It would later be established that Fowler and Watson had emerged from the woods below the schoolhouse and walked to the building.

The two were later seen in the yard of Dr. Bramblett where, it is speculated, they had planned to lure him into his office, administer fatal blows, and steal his automobile, which he kept in good running condition for visits to patients.

During the days that followed, a strong case was building against Watson and Fowler. On the afternoon of the robbery, Watson had been arrested at his home. He had then led investigators to Roper's empty wallet where it had been tossed into a creek.

Fowler, however, fled first to Atlanta, from Atlanta to Knoxville, Tennessee in an automobile, then from Knoxville to Louisville, Kentucky, and on to Bardstown, Kentucky in a different automobile. A woman named Ethel Wade had traveled with him as far as Louisville. Finally, Fowler was arrested in Cincinnati—for the kidnapping of a Baptist minister in Kentucky—and extradited to Georgia.

The trial that ensued, known as *The State* v. *Walter Fowler and Austin Watson*, case #1915, began on May 5, 1943. Witnesses in the case established the whereabouts of the defendants on the day of the robbery: Between 9 a.m. and 10 a.m. on Monday, February 22, declared M.M. Green, the duo came into his store on Canton Highway and bought soft drinks. Fowler was clad in overalls and the shirt to his Marine uniform. At about 11:30 a.m., they returned to Green's Store. At that time, Fowler was wearing his Marine uniform. After a brief stop with no purchases, both departed in the direction of Cuba and Ben Roper's Store.

Mrs. Roy Redd, Ben Roper's daughter, recalled seeing Watson and Fowler pass her house, located near her father's store, between 11:30 and noon while she was

Benjamin Roper's four children were, from left to right, (front row) Kate and Frank, and (back row) Alyce and Mac.

listening to a radio program. Fowler, she remembered, was wearing his Marine uniform. Then, in 30 or 40 minutes, she learned of her father's injuries.

Ben Roper's son Mack testified as to his father's account of the robbery and beating given when he regained consciousness at Georgia Baptist Hospital:

> He said he couldn't live, that they had killed him. I asked him who it was. He said that Austin Watson and his brother-in-law Fowler came in the store and Watson wanted some candy and he went back to the candy case and gave him the candy, and Fowler then wanted a Coca Cola. So he got him the Coca Cola. Then they turned around to pay him for it, so he reached in his left pocket to get the change, and he had bent over to take it out, and they hit him and knocked him to his knees. He didn't say at that point which one of them hit him first. He said he got back up and they had a nice "rassle," but he said there was too many of them, and he said after that one of them hit him and the other one taken the money off him. He said that Watson hit him with the hatchet and that Fowler hit him with the gun.

Other witnesses followed. Presenting a compelling case against Fowler and Watson, these witnesses convinced the jury of the guilt of both. Fowler was sentenced to be executed on June 25, 1943. Following the appeal process, Fowler's sentence was carried out on March 2, 1945. As fate would have it, Austin Watson, handed down a life sentence, would die about three months after Fowler's execution in a prison fire where he was incarcerated at Ben Hill in Southwest Atlanta. Years later, a suggested link between the prison fire and the deadly Winecoff Hotel fire in Atlanta in 1946 hinted that the two blazes may have been started by the same individual.

Maggie Tribble Roper, widow of Ben Roper, stands in the yard in front of the Roper house. The store was to the right of the house.

7. Schools and Educators

That Forsyth County has been committed to the education of her youth has been apparent from the early days of the old field school to the institutions of learning today. As the land was cleared and the essentials were assured—as much as anything can be certain in an agrarian society—the citizens of yore began a system of education to prepare youngsters for the future. Field schools could be found scattered throughout the area, for paved roads and school buses would be a phenomenon of the twentieth century and beyond. Children of the nineteenth century would have to walk through mud or dust to their neighborhood one- or two-room school.

Well into the twentieth century, conditions were basically the same. Hightower School or "Frogtown" as it was known colloquially, is a prime example. The building itself and the teaching methods and materials belonged to the historic era. In the classrooms, long benches sufficed for seating except for a few desks. At one end of the room was an area set aside for recitations. As the teacher, "Miss Ruth" Hawkins, later Mrs. Eugene Wallace, worked directly with a group of students in this section, others not momentarily involved in recitations would quietly assist younger children with their lessons. Using textbooks either purchased or handed down from child to child within families, the youngsters at Frogtown transported their books to and from the classroom in flour sack book bags.

Modern conveniences being unknown, sticks supported the school's open windows during warm weather and, in lieu of running water, the older boys in the class toted water from the house across the road. Water from a bucket and dipper was the forerunner of the present-day water fountain.

Work did not prevail for the entire school day. During recess periods, youngsters channeled their energy into a vigorous game of tag or Red Rover. Playground equipment being an unheard-of luxury, students used their imaginations in playing together with classmates. The girls often constructed playhouses in the dirt schoolyard.

Perhaps the most popular recess school game was Antney Over, played with a team on opposite sides of the school building. The team with the ball would call "Antney." The other team would respond with "over," at which time the ball would be hurled across the schoolhouse. The player catching the ball would scoot

Frogtown School was typical of the rural educational setting. Classes were held on the first floor, while the second floor served as an Oddfellow Lodge.

around the building and tag as many opposing team members as possible. Each child tagged would then become a member of the team with the ball. And how was the game won? When all of the players were converted to one side, that team was declared victorious.

Besides being the location for high-spirited fun, the schoolyard also served as the dining area, weather permitting. Lunchtime found most students outside devouring the contents of their lard buckets while they awaited the return of those few individuals who lived close enough to eat dinner at home. Baked sweet potatoes and jelly biscuits were considered an adequate meal in those days.

In the wintertime, though, pupils clustered around a pot-bellied stove, which was kept fueled through the efforts of parents in the community and children alike. The parents provided the wood while the boys gathered the needed kindling. Before the students could enjoy the warmth of the stove and the cheerful, cooperative atmosphere of the classroom, however, they had to brave the adverse conditions of the unpaved Old Federal Road, which passed in front of the school, and the frequently high waters of unbridged creeks in the vicinity. Walking was the mode of travel, except when Wilson Pruitt would haul students in his 1939 pickup, adapted with a wooden body on the back.

The body of the truck was not the only "body" of interest to the pupils. Horace Whitmire recalls that he and some of the older boys would slip up the stairs to the

Odd Fellow Lodge, which occupied the second story of the schoolhouse. There they would view the skeleton that the fraternal order used in its initiations. To a young lad, being scared out of his wits was a wonderfully exciting experience. Whitmire, who entered Frogtown in 1943, related that his teacher was Flora Belle Wallis and that Evelyn Heard, the teacher in grades six through nine, was also the principal. But what happened in a two-room school when one of the teachers was sick? Why, the neighbors helped out. Mrs. Yarbrough from across the road would come and teach classes until almost dinner time. Then her husband Charlie would arrive to sit with the children while his wife went to tend to the cooking. The noon meal completed, Mrs. Yarbrough would resume the day's lessons.

The saga of the old wooden schoolhouses remained the same for decades. It was not until well into the twentieth century that buildings were updated and a larger number of pupils were taught under one roof. Such was the story of Friendship School in the settlement known as Cuba. Friendship began as a small wooden school next to Friendship Church. When the need arose, an addition was constructed adjacent to the old building. Subsequently, this "complex" was destroyed by fire and it was imperative for the community to have a new school to take its place.

The new brick building, funded through bonds, was a fine structure for the 1940s and members of the community took great pride in their impressive educational institution. When the new Friendship opened in the fall of 1947, a PTA was formed with Mrs. Joe Bramblett being elected president and Mrs. Luther Karr as secretary. A committee composed of the teachers, Mrs. Joe Heard, and Mrs. Luster Dishroom was appointed to solicit funds for auditorium seating.

This photo shows Friendship School as it existed in the 1950s. A lunchroom was later added on the right end of the building.

Education progressed more or less uneventfully at Friendship until May 1961 when a fire raged through the building. According to the *Atlanta Constitution*, more than 200 pupils evacuated the structure at about 10:30 a.m. as fire popped and crackled in the attic overhead. The school's fire alarm having failed to work, two students ran from classroom to classroom to warn teachers and students of the danger. Miriam Sosebee, the teacher who discovered the blaze, is credited with these remarks: "They [the students] were all just as calm as could be. I was outside during my recess when I saw black smoke pouring through the ventilators in the top of the building. . . . The fire had cut off all electricity and we sent two students around to warn the others."

A slightly different version of the story, appearing in the *Gainesville Times*, indicated that the cooks, preparing the third meal to be served in the new cafetorium, heard a noise in the attic and reported the fire. Principal B.J. Brookshire immediately called a routine fire drill and 170 pupils walked to safety. Brookshire reported that he then summoned the Cumming Fire Department, who prevented the fire from spreading. School Superintendent Almon Hill estimated that all the wiring would have to be replaced, along with repairs to the rafters. The new lunchroom, which had been recently added, received the lion's share of the damage.

Ironically, the fine brick Friendship building was utilized for only about 20 years. Just as the bonds that enabled the construction of the building were finally paid off, the school was consolidated with Ducktown and Matt schools, and pupils were sent to the new Sawnee Elementary in the fall of 1968.

The history of Ducktown School closely parallels that of Friendship—sans fire. From wooden structures in the vicinity to a brick building erected and furnished through the efforts of its patrons, Ducktown served as an elementary school until its consolidation with Friendship and Matt, and its pupils were transported to Sawnee in 1968. Unlike Friendship and Matt, however, Ducktown continued to be utilized for educational purposes after the consolidation, with Head Start and kindergarten housed within its walls.

The final school that is representative of the trend of the latter half of the twentieth century—that of busing students for miles across the county to a consolidated institution consisting of a larger building and greater number of pupils—is Matt. Matt was considered "Matt High School" when it was completed in 1945 because it housed students in grades one through eight. By modern standards, though, it was an elementary school.

In its early years, Matt School was a typical wooden rural building, located on Elmo Road in close proximity to Hurt and Moore's Store on the site now occupied by Leon's at Bannister Road and Highway 369.

Grades one through nine were taught there until December 1942 when the school was destroyed by fire. In the interim, while a new building was being erected, classes were held in Zion Hill church with Maggie Worley teaching the primary group and Louise Walls with the older students. Incidentally, Worley, with an incomplete teaching certificate, earned $2 per day during this period. Also of note, she taught all four of her daughters—Lewellen, Sue, Nancy, and Barbara—as they began their formal education.

Although the school had been in use since 1945, the cornerstone for the new brick Matt School was laid in 1948 with J. Clayton Perry, Grand Master of Georgia Masons, conducting the ceremony. A.R. Housley was school superintendent of Forsyth County. H.T. Pirkle, A.W. Harris, J.W. Tatum, J.M. Corn, I.L. Wallis, M.E. Jennings, and Olen Sexton served as trustees.

The building of Matt School coincided with the activities of the Community Improvement Club, which was organized after the chicken industry had raised the standard of living in Forsyth County and citizens were seeking ways to improve the area in which they resided. The spirit carried over to the school and many projects, such as landscaping the exterior, were a part of the organization's agenda. Yet, everything wasn't modern at Matt. Indoor plumbing was still in the future and discipline was still strict. A "whupping" at school meant another licking at home.

Improvements may have come slowly, but come they did. While Ford Phillips was principal, a very active PTA urged Lois Heard and Jewell Jennings to start a lunchroom. The cafeteria thus established was not only equipped with trays and dishes begged from the Henry Grady Hotel and S & W Cafeteria in Atlanta, but it boasted a coal-burning army range as well. To supplement store-bought food, the lunchroom staff prepared turnip greens, beans, tomatoes, and other vegetables from the school's own garden.

Recollections have been shared by former students, teachers, and patrons. For example, Marie Groover related that she came to Matt as a substitute teacher for two or three days and ended up teaching for two years. Then, Wilda Bailey recalled the excellent school plays written by Ruth Wallace and performed by various students. Bailey was also impressed by the support given by the PTA for the carnival, the willingness of Redger Worley and Guerney Whitmire to clean the lunchroom afterward, and the late night sessions of counting the proceeds on the shag rug in her home.

The years 1967 and 1968 marked the last term school held at Matt, for, the succeeding year, students joined others from Ducktown and Friendship at the new consolidated Sawnee Elementary. Matt's final staff consisted of Maggie Worley, Dot Otwell, Flora Belle Wallis, Lois Heard, Eunice Williams, and Ruth Wallace, with Alton Treadaway serving as principal.

From the country to town, education in Cumming was somewhat different from the one or two teacher rural schools. In 1839, the Forsyth County Academy, later to be known as the Cumming Academy, was erected where the present-day Tolbert Street crosses Maple Street. The school was affiliated with the Masonic fraternity. Records of LaFayette Masonic Lodge #44 F&AM indicate that a new brick lodge hall and academy was to be ready for occupancy by August 1856.

Legislation by the state of Georgia in 1858 to establish a common school system significantly impacted educational planning in Forsyth County, as evidenced by the Grand Jury presentments in February 1859. But scarcely had the Grand Jury devised its plan for complying with the new law than the Civil War precipitated the abandonment of most academic endeavors throughout the south, Forsyth County included. Alas, no records of lodge or educational activities are available for the years 1859 to 1865, as both lodge and school remained suspended during the war years.

Then, in December 1865, the academy building was renovated, once again put into use, and rented to various teachers who attempted to educate the youth of the town while staying within a reasonable budget for the lean times.

By 1873, the term "Cumming High School" began to appear in the minutes of the lodge. Colonel Hiram Parks Bell offered a resolution to rent the building to the trustees of Cumming High School. This arrangement continued until 1883 and, again, there is a skip in the records—to 1891.

Meanwhile, other educational endeavors captured the spotlight, for Piedmont College was erected on what is now known as School Street just north of the town square in 1888. The "college" actually wasn't an institution of higher learning at all, but a school that offered a high school curriculum. As with the old academy, the Masons were once again in the business of education. In this structure, the lodge hall was situated on the right end of the second floor and the school classes were held downstairs. Cumming's newspaper *The Clarion* reported the following on March 9, 1888:

Members of the 4-H Club posed in front of the Matt School building erected in 1945. The school was closed in 1968 when Matt was consolidated with two other schools to form the new Sawnee Elementary.

The institution known through the years as Piedmont College, Hightower Baptist College, and Hightower Baptist Institute provided a high school curriculum for students in the Cumming area.

> The entrance examination was held last week and the following students were admitted as freshmen: Bell Clement, Cliff Lester, Victoria Hockenhull, Ada Sims, Lillie Mullino, Clara McGinness, Fannie Eakes, Charles Foster, Fred Mullino, James Hockenhull, Paul Clement, Thomas J. Pirkle and R.M. Hughes, all having obtained over 85 per cent.

A few years later, a religious group entered the picture. The report of a meeting of the Hightower Baptist Association indicated that the delegates recognized the need for a denominational high school in the Forsyth County area. Shortly thereafter, plans for the Hightower Baptist College evolved into reality. On August 10, 1893, the newspaper *The Baptist Leader* offered a detailed account of the events pursuant to the opening of the facility:

> More than a year ago this school seemed uncertain and the outlook gloomy.
>
> At a meeting of the Hightower Association, held at Mount Vernon last August, an executive committee consisting of brethren W.J. Hyde, H.I. Foster, A.C. Conn, J.T. Reese and Joel Webb, was appointed to meet in Cumming in October together with a delegate from each church in the association, to locate and establish this school.

These brethren met and three or four locations were made and after considerable discussion, Cumming was selected as the location.

The school was located and it was decided that the building known as Piedmont College should be purchased. Time went on, until near the last of November and nothing had been done more than selecting a location. The Executive Committee got together then and elected Rev. A.E. Booth President and agent for the institution.

He went to work and . . . was able to put the school into operation Jan. 2, 1893. On December 31, the Executive Committee met and bought the property from the Trustees of Piedmont College, and deeds to the property were made, and on the next Monday morning 80 pupils were present. The patronage increased until at the close of the past term nearly 200 pupils had been enrolled, representing seven counties and states.

Throughout the 1890s, the Hightower Baptist Institute boasted a substantial enrollment from the primary grades through high school. During the 1895–1896 term, the school staff consisted of J.G. Harrison, president and high school teacher; E.H. Holland, vice president and assistant high school teacher; Miss Sallie Newton, intermediate grades; Miss Nettie White, primary grades; and E.C. White, music director.

Beginning in 1907, the trustees of Cumming School District utilized the school building of the Hightower Baptist Institute to house Cumming elementary and high school pupils and teachers. In 1908, T.P. Tribble was listed as teacher for Cumming School. Lela Bishop and Lou Rhodes were enumerated as assistants to Tribble in 1909.

The old Piedmont College/Hightower Baptist Institute building served the educational needs of Cumming District until it was declared unfit and students were sent home on short notice. Then, a new brick school was erected in 1923 by J.W. Fleming, who fired the bricks for the edifice at his brick yard on the site of the present city parking lot across from Goodson Drugs.

As fate would have it, this structure was destroyed by fire after being in use for only a short duration. Lightning had struck near the roof on the back side of the building in March 1927. Subsequently, Fleming was again pressed into service and the school was rebuilt "within the same walls" and opened to students in the fall of 1927. It should be noted that, had Dr. Marcus Mashburn Sr., a school trustee, not paid the insurance premium himself, the money would not have been available to replace the 1923 school that burned. By 1930, a roster of students for Forsyth County recorded Cumming School with a total enrollment of 305 pupils. In the elementary grades, 189 were listed, and for high school, 116.

To Cumming students, their academic standing was of utmost importance. In November 1927, "first honors" were accorded: Wendell Bramblett, Ada Spence, Anna Leene Bramblett, Gladyse Smith, and Nellie Kate Wallace—11th grade; Viola Holcomb, Minnie Lou Hawkins, and Ralph Pirkle—tenth grade;

Ida Mae Hammond, Montree Thompson, Ruby Collins, Ado Gage, and Louise Hawks—ninth grade; Mary Jo Hawkins, Esta Lee Holbrook, Zella Johnson, Lucille Tollison, Gladyse Kennemore, Sara Bess Clement, and Helen Keller—eighth grade; Bettie Lee Wheeler, Edward Patterson, John D. Glover, and Mary Frances Barrett—seventh grade; James Ivy Hughes—sixth grade; Ralph Holbrook and James Otwell—fifth grade; and Edna Kennemore, Willie Lou Stephens, Laura Ruth Webb, and Charles Bettis—fourth grade.

Cumming School continued to serve pupils in grades one through high school-age until the Forsyth County High School on Tribble Gap Road opened in 1955. Then, Cumming Lower Elementary School on Elm Street began classes in 1961. Only the middle grades remained at the old school, which was known during its final years as an educational institution as Cumming Upper Elementary.

Students were no longer housed within Cumming School's brick walls after Otwell Middle School was established. As the Upper Elementary's final days were drawing to a close, three of the last administrators to serve as principal included a Mr. Adelotte, Garland Shoemake, and James Hester. Hester transferred to Otwell, as that school's first principal, with the students from Cumming at the conclusion of the 1973–1974 school term.

Lest one believe that Cumming School was abandoned with the removal of the student body to Otwell, the record must be set straight. In the summer of 1974, the building was converted from a schoolhouse to administrative offices for the Forsyth County schools. By September of that year, the superintendent's office was settled under Cumming's roof. Then, amid the interior remodeling in progress, the other county school personnel joined the superintendent one by one.

Today, the school system's proliferating county staff no longer operates from the structure that has influenced the lives of numerous Forsyth Countians, but numerous Cumming alumni retain memories of their years in the stately brick structure with the Gothic parapet.

Rupert Bramblett attended Cumming School in the seventh grade and during his high school years, and graduated in 1937. This 83-year-old retired physician remembers well the forms of discipline imposed on the student population to maintain proper decorum. In addition to being spanked or having the principal visit one's father, a junior or senior could expect to be detained after school for an infraction of the school rules. And while this unruly pupil was "serving his time," he was required to march around the building while carrying a piece of lumber carved to resemble a gun. The teacher in charge of monitoring the punishment was stationed near a front window to observe the offender as he passed by the school's facade.

An effective form of discipline? Maybe not. Frequently, as the marcher rounded the building, he would run at top speed to the other side, take a few puffs on a cigarette, exchange a quick anecdote with a fellow marcher, assume a solemn countenance, and again parade by in view of the teacher. One of the favorite songs on the forced marches admonished the listener to:

Cumming School was erected in 1923, burned in March 1927, and was rebuilt by September 1927. The structure is currently owned by the City of Cumming.

Take me back to Colorado,
She's a-beatin' old Nevada,
How I'm longin' for them foothills everyday,
It's so soothin' in the evenin'
When the old gray wolf's a-grievin'.
Take me back to Colorado for-to-stay!

Montree Hansard Martin, who attended Cumming in grades eight through eleven, remembers school from a different perspective from that of discipline. She relates that the times were so relaxed that pupils could leave school and go to town for a Coca-Cola at the drug store during their lunch breaks.

Ruth Hawkins Wallace, who attended Cumming School in grades five through high school, returned as a sixth grade teacher during the war years (1942 to 1945). "Miss Ruth," who rode the school bus from her home at Coal Mountain to Cumming everyday, had an anxiety-producing experience once on the last day of school. She had forgotten to bring her pupils' report cards! After a brief panic, she realized that it was essential to find someone with gasoline ration coupons or she would have to go the distance back home on foot as a result of her oversight. Walk she didn't. Helen Fowler came to the rescue with coupons for enough gasoline to drive to Coal Mountain and back!

Marie Bagley Roper recalled that World War II created strange situations in the educational setting. At the beginning of the war, she was teaching at Friendship School and there she wished to remain. But it was not to be, as the Board of

Education "drafted" her to teach at Cumming. Given her choice of subjects, she opted to teach ninth grade history and eighth grade health, but that's not all. She and Helen Brooks were placed in charge of the Victory Corps, a group of girls who were to emulate soldiers by wearing uniforms, exercising, and marching. The parents of that day accepted the exercising and marching considerably better than they did the uniforms, which resembled bloomers.

Clara Mae Redd Cox's memories of the old school are numerous and varied—from someone beating on radiators to extract heat to eating lunch outside the building when the weather was favorable. On April Fools Day, Cox recalls, almost everyone would leave school. So few remained that school would be turned out for the day. On one such occasion, laden with books and overcoat, she went to town and attempted unsuccessfully to find a ride home. She and several others in the same predicament began the four-mile trek toward Cuba, Georgia. Luckily, a bus driver met the weary group near Sawnee Mountain and provided transportation to their homes.

During Cox's senior year, Perry Holbrook sold his school bus and left approximately seven students with no way to and from Cumming. The group solved its dilemma, though, by tightly packing themselves into a car driven by Evelyn Padgett and riding "sardine style" for about 25¢ per week.

The rough spots tended to balance out. For example, while Cox was sitting around a table with mischievous girls in the library—the location of Ruth

Clara Mae Redd Cox attended Friendship School in her youth and later taught in the brick building constructed in the late 1940s. She finished her career at Sawnee Elementary.

Wallace's government class—Miss Ruth looked at the others and said, "You girls stop that. You're a bad influence on Clara Mae."

There was an unexpected challenge near the end of Cox's senior year after she had been chosen class valedictorian. In typing class, the old ribbon on the typewriter stopped functioning properly and the teacher declared, "Anybody who is going to be valedictorian should be able to put a ribbon on a typewriter." Cox had never seen anyone install a new ribbon, much less attempted it herself. As the teacher adamantly refused to let classmates proffer suggestions or assist with the task, the valedictorian demonstrated her problem-solving ability. The ribbon was finally placed correctly and typing lessons resumed.

Dorothy Otwell taught first grade at Cumming from 1954 until 1961, when Cumming Lower Elementary on Elm Street opened. During her first year (1954–1955), all grades were housed at Cumming School, but the following year, the high school moved to its new plant on Tribble Gap Road.

Practicality was in evidence on a day-to-day basis at Cumming School. Otwell's class, which ordinarily went outside and around the building to enter the lunchroom, would stoop down and negotiate the crawl space beneath the building to avoid the elements during periods of inclement weather. Quite an adventure for the little folks!

Don Shadburn instructed seventh and eighth grade students in history, English, math, and science at Cumming Upper Elementary from 1965 to 1968, when he transferred to Sawnee Elementary. From a student's perspective, Shadburn recollects that grades one through seven were contained in a white building behind the main brick structure, which at that time was used for the seventh and eighth grades. In the basement of the brick building were two elementary classrooms. His teacher for Farm and Home Living was Lanier Bannister, who controlled his classes in the small white building behind the school by striking students across the legs with long sticks. Later, as an educator himself, Shadburn taught one year in a tiny, narrow room under the lunchroom. This classroom featured an oil burning heater, two long rows of desks, a door to the outside, and about 25 pupils.

During Robert Otwell's years as county school superintendent, he collected desks and other academic memorabilia in anticipation of a time when these reminders of education in the "olden days" could be displayed for future generations. An exhibit of this type, he believed, would give youngsters an insight into their heritage.

The story of education in Forsyth County would not be complete without the recognition of several outstanding educators, including Minnie Bailey Julian, who resided on the Dawson–Forsyth County line. The late Garland Bagley was known to have frequently declared that this lady was the "Martha Berry of our area." Having arrived at the Julian farm shortly after her marriage to Abijah John Julian, Minnie Bailey Julian visited a nearby school, Mount Nebo, and that visit clinched her decision to make the teaching profession her life's work. In the fall of 1865, she opened her first school in a former slave cabin and continued to teach at various schools for the next 35 years. In 1881, she was instrumental in establishing Chestatee High School—also known as the Julian School. But a change was in store. In 1885, Minnie Julian relocated to the old Gainesville College, where she taught English. Yet, her career in education did not end there, for in 1891, she was appointed by Governor Northern to the Board of Visitors to the Normal and Industrial College of Millegeville.

From the Drew community, Miss Fannie Harrell embarked on a career that was to be short-lived, but noteworthy nevertheless. An intellectually gifted individual, "Miss Fannie" attended LaGrange Female College where she was class prophet in the graduating class of June 7, 1893. Subsequently, she received her master's degree from Columbia University and departed for Puerto Rico, where she boarded with the former governor and taught English. A few years later, she taught in Miami and Bradenton, Florida. Her teaching career also included a brief period in the Forsyth County schools, but ended after the death of her mother in 1910, when Miss Fannie remained on the Forsyth County farm to care for her ailing father, Newton Harrell, and to help manage the farm and the family's business interests.

Stella Benson Bell also distinguished herself in the field of education. Having been educated in the local schools and having attended the Hightower Baptist Institute at Cumming, Stella Bell then taught at a number of county schools, including Brandywine, Harris Grove, Silver Shoals, Antioch, and Salem. Moreover, she was active in civic, social, and religious life wherever she worked.

A "first" in Forsyth County, claimed by Bell, was quite a feat. Not only was she the first woman to learn to drive a car—no small accomplishment—but she learned to control the automobile on unpaved and sometimes treacherous roads. It is likely that, being an avid horsewoman, she considered the cars of her day only one level above the equines she treasured dearly. A certain level of self-confidence would have been a prerequisite for managing both animal and machine.

The reader should not assume that only women were great educators. Men, such as Arthur Monroe Sosebee, left their mark, too. A teacher to the core, Sosebee, born on June 19, 1891, attended the public schools of Forsyth County—Sweeney, Barrett, and Tallant—and finished grammar school at Mt. Pisgah. Later having graduated with a high school diploma from Reinhardt Normal School and with third grade teaching certificate in hand, he embarked on a teaching career that was to span 50 years.

Edith Sosebee Wright in *Golden Memories* described her father's educational pursuits and the jobs he undertook to support a wife—the former Beulah Inez Wallis, whom he married in 1912—and five daughters:

> Mr. Sosebee resigned his teaching position at Friendship Junior High in October, 1923 to work in the Post Office in the Old Federal Building in Atlanta, Georgia. In early January, 1924, he moved his family to Waleska, Georgia to live in a dormitory at Reinhardt College as house parent. Just before Martha was to be born in 1927, the Sosebees moved into a

house near the college. In the fall of 1925, Mr. Sosebee became a teacher at Waleska Elementary and a student at Reinhardt College. During the next two years he worked as a barber on Saturday and after school. He also harvested four bales of cotton in the dry year of 1925.

Upon completion of two years college education at Reinhardt College, Mr. Sosebee and family returned to Forsyth County to begin teaching again at Friendship Junior High in 1927. Mr. Sosebee taught either as principal, teacher or both at Friendship . . . for a total of 21 years. While teaching, Mr. Sosebee continued to take extension courses in education from the University of Georgia. He commuted for almost two years to Oglethorpe University, where he received his B.A. in Education in 1941.

Years later in his career, in fact, the year of his retirement, Arthur Sosebee received a distinct honor when his student Lamar Orr, named Star Student, selected him as Star Teacher on February 16, 1961. At the end of that school term, Sosebee retired from Forsyth County High School, but not from education altogether, for he continued to teach basic adult education classes and to substitute at Matt, Midway, Sawnee, and Forsyth County High School.

Another well known gentleman, Almon C. Hill, born on December 1, 1905, distinguished himself not only as a teacher, but as a coach as well. Hill was born in

Fannie Harrell taught in Florida and in Puerto Rico as well as in Forsyth County. She later gave up her teaching career to care for her sick parents.

the Heardsville community of Forsyth County, attended Friendship School, and graduated from Cumming High School in 1925. In pursuit of higher learning, he earned a degree from Oglethorpe University in 1940 and was awarded a master's degree in Administration from the University of Georgia in 1962. He was married to the late Fairy Tribble Hill for 58 years.

Almon Hill's career began in 1926 when he taught at Ducktown Elementary School. Then he worked in the elementary schools through 1934 and thereafter served as a teacher, principal, and coach at Friendship and Bethelview Junior High Schools until 1942. Hill is probably best remembered for his years at Cumming High School and Forsyth County High School, 1942 through 1956, when he taught and coached baseball and basketball. Indeed, his teams were the envy of the region.

Rest on his laurels as a teacher and winning coach? Not Almon Hill. The remainder of his 54 years of service in the Forsyth County Schools were spent as county school superintendent, 1957 to 1969; member of the Forsyth County Board of Education, 1973 to 1980; and a substitute teacher for 10 years. Hill garnered numerous honors and awards during his years in education. As County School Superintendent, he held several offices in the Ninth District, but sports were his forte, as evidenced by his being designated Coach of the Year in Region 4 basketball in the Ninth District in 1953 and Coach of the Year in Class B Georgia basketball in 1954. His girls basketball team played in seven consecutive state tournaments, while the boys team played in four. In addition, Hill was recognized as a member of the Hubie Smith's Sixth Man Club in 1979 by the Atlanta Hawks, elected to the Sports Trail Century Club in 1952, *Who's Who in American Education* in 1963, and *Who's Who in South/Southwest* in 1963–1964.

Almon Hill was a teacher and winning basketball coach in Forsyth County. His wife Fairy also taught school for decades in Forsyth County.

8. Tragedy and Inspiration

Forsyth County has witnessed both turbulent times and those which seemed ideal for accomplishment. Perhaps it has taken both tragedy and inspiration for the history of the county to evolve and for progress to take place, for out of tragedy has sprung hope, and out of hope, inspiration.

An example of individuals whose spirit would not be suppressed is the intertwined story of Cicero Anglin, Dolly Bagley and a house. The story began to unfold when Cicero Anglin, born in 1839 and married to Clarinda Wilson in 1860, returned from the Civil War with a dream. Lean times at home did not quench the desire of this young man to erect a magnificent house and farm for his family. Indeed, through diligent efforts, Anglin, in 1887, became the owner of a magnificent Folk Victorian structure that was the envy of the community. The Anglins resided in their fine home from that time until Clarinda passed away, *c.* 1912, and Anglin sold the house and went to live with his daughter and son-in-law Sarah and Albert Matthew Bell, until his death in 1927.

End of the story? Absolutely not. Another young person, Clarence "Dolly" Bagley entered the picture long before the Anglin house was sold. Elisha Bagley, Dolly's father, had died *c.* 1871, leaving a wife and one son. Widowed at a young age and with a child to raise, Eliza Jane Brannon Bagley eked out an existence as well as she could under the circumstances. With no public assistance to fall back on in those days, Elisha Bagley's widow admirably survived the lean years as her son Dolly emerged from infancy on the journey to manhood.

Along that journey—an incident in the road, so to speak—young Dolly acquired a dream, which would be the focus of his endeavors for years to come. At about eight years of age, the lad had raised a calf and was carrying the hide to the tannery, some four or five miles from his home, when he beheld a new house, the Cicero Anglin home, under construction. The dwelling was the most splendid he had ever seen and he was utterly captivated! Indeed, his aspirations would never be the same after that moment.

Dolly continued on to the tannery and completed the intended transaction. With the 25¢ he received for the calf hide, he had a variety of options. As he stepped into a nearby store, the allure of candy must have been enticing. Did he spend his money for his own gratification? No, for a small blue bowl caught his eye. Just the thing for his mother to serve gravy in! The decision was clinched, the bowl purchased, and the unselfish boy turned homeward.

Upon his return, the bowl and the story of his dream were simultaneously bestowed upon his mother. Near the tannery was the largest house he had ever seen. Adamantly, young Dolly proclaimed that someday he would own that house and that farm. Years later, he did.

A dream by itself is just a dream. In Dolly Bagley's psyche, however, the 10 percent inspiration became coupled with the 90 percent perspiration required for its fulfillment, and his efforts toward that end extended into the following decade and beyond. Never relinquishing hope, Dolly held on tenaciously to his ambition to own the stately Folk Victorian structure erected by Cicero Anglin.

Clarence C. "Dolly" Bagley and Creola Augusta Scales, the daughter of Willis F. and Nancy Bagby Scales, were married on October 12, 1908 at Island Ford Church in Gwinnett County, Georgia. On August 4, 1909, their son Garland was born, followed by daughter Blanche on November 26, 1910. Then began the realization of the dream, for when Garland was three years old and Blanche two, the Dolly Bagleys moved into the magnificent dwelling that had so impressed the youngster years before. And not long thereafter, the third and final child of the Bagleys was born in the Victorian "dream house" graced with Gothic elements. Marie Bagley arrived on April 20, 1916 in beautiful surroundings on a farm that would eventually encompass 160 acres.

But not all tales have a storybook ending as the Bagley plot. Sadly, Susie Harrell's is one of them. Susie was a radiant flower plucked from our midst—slowly,

The house built by Cicero Anglin and later acquired by Clarence "Dolly" Bagley was an impressive Folk Victorian.

agonizingly, petal by petal, ebullient spirit wilted and sere, until finally the stem was snapped and the break was forever. Such is the nature of mental illness. Unlike a fatal accident where the scene can be viewed or the terminal illness of which the etiology is known, the mental deterioration of the schizophrenic extols a devastation on family and friends that is unique in its amalgam of violent eruptions, dashed hopes, failed cures, and family shame and disruption.

The Harrells of Forsyth County experienced the gamut of emotions as their youngest child Susie—bright, attractive, and talented—succumbed to the ravages of an affliction that would persist throughout her long life. Alas, neither the miracle drugs nor the skill of modern day psychiatry were available in the first two decades of the twentieth century when her illness could no longer be managed at home.

The road to the abysmal depths of despair is Susie's story.

Susie descended from a family who arrived in Forsyth County c. 1835, along with Edward Harrell's wife's brothers, the Stricklands. Remaining just long enough to establish a productive farm, which would today be accorded the term "agribusiness," Edward and his wife were drawn to the gold fields of California. Their son Newton, however, unable to tolerate the western climate, returned to the plantation on the Post Road in the western section of the county and raised his family in the stately home erected by his father.

On February 11, 1858, Newton Harrell married Mary Ellender Harris, the daughter of Lorenzo Dow Harris. Seven offspring were born to this couple, including Susie, born on January 3, 1877. Little is known of Susie Harrell's early years, except for the environment in which she was raised. The Harrells, being a cultured people, were wont to travel and to avail themselves of all the educational advantages at their disposal. More affluent than the average Forsyth Countians of their day, they could offer opportunities to enrich the lives of their children. In religion, the Harrells were affiliated with the Holbrook Campground and the Methodist church nearby.

That Susie was an intellectually gifted young lady is evidenced by her graduation from La Grange Female College in 1894—at the age of 17! Her sister Fanny had graduated from the same institution just one year earlier. Subsequent to graduation, Susie pursued a career in education by accepting a teaching position at nearby Bethlehem School. In 1896, she taught the summer term at Settles School in the southeastern section of the county.

In addition to teaching, Susie had other aspirations as well. She completed a year of study at the School of Expression in Boston, Massachusetts and, on May 11, 1901, received a glowing recommendation from that school's registrar, Anna B. Curry. Not only did Harrell receive praise in academic circles, but she captured the attention of the community where she resided—known as Drew—as well. Her flower garden and summer house on the Harrell plantation received wide acclaim, with friends and neighbors delighting in the beauty of her efforts.

From such a scene of promise, one's first inclination is to ask, "What went wrong?" The illness that caused the deterioration of the woman who appeared to have the world at her command remains a mystery. One can only sadly examine the results.

The exact time of the onset of Harrell's illness is uncertain. However, her parents, prior to their deaths, spared no expense in seeking assistance for their youngest child. Unfortunately, her mother died in 1910, broken hearted that Susie's condition had not improved. Susie's sister Fannie then returned to the home place from Puerto Rico to care for their father Newton, who passed away in 1912.

Lest the curious reader wonder as to the manifestations of Susie's illness, a few incidences may be cited. Prior to the start of her aberrant behavior, Newton Harrell had admonished his daughter not to attempt to drive a certain horse into town because the animal tended to be skittish and might bolt out of control. Nevertheless, determined and undeterred by her father's warning, Susie set out for Cumming at the lines of the questionable equine. Alas, Newton's prophetic words came to pass, for the horse "went wild," upset the buggy, and unceremoniously dumped Susie on her head. Some members of the family attributed the change in Susie's behavior to the head injury she received in the accident. Others vehemently denied that the horse and buggy episode was a contributing factor at all. This latter group held that the practice of intermarriage of first cousins in the family for generations was responsible. Even her sister Fanny decried the close family marriages, but did not go so far as to apply the genetic concept to her sister's condition. Capable financial managers, the Harrells knew without a doubt that something was wrong when they discovered Susie Harrell burning money. Their attention—and horror—were captured. It is likely that this is the incident that mobilized the family into seeking professional assistance.

After the death of her parents, Susie's mental deterioration continued. The situation reached a climax when Susie became violent and attempted to take the life of her brother Charley. Cognizant that all treatments had failed and that the family could no longer care for their hopelessly ill sibling at home, the Harrells sought the assistance of the county. A panel of 18 men were summoned and commanded to assemble at the home of C.N. (Charley) Harrell at 10:00 on January 23, 1917 for a lunacy trial. A jury of six was selected. In summary, the records declare the final verdict: " . . . we find Miss Susie Harrell to be violently insane and fit for the sanitarium . . . (signed) John H. Hockenhull, T.A. Creamer, S.W. Hawkins, W.C. Wheeler, A.H. Westbrook, W.F. Westbrook." Court orders for Susie's commitment to the sanitarium at Millegeville were signed by W.J. Tidwell, Ordinary.

When Newton Harrell passed away in 1912, he left a sizable estate to be divided among his six living offspring. To receive her share, which amounted to around $7,000 paid out over a number of years as notes came due from debtors, Susie's situation necessitated the appointment of a guardian. On February 12, 1917, her sister Fanny received the appointment from W.J. Tidwell. Regardless of the well known sibling rivalry and bad feelings between Susie and Fanny, nevertheless,

Susie Harrell, the brilliant daughter of Newton Harrell, fell prey to mental illness from which she never recovered.

Fanny utilized her astute business acumen to manage the Susie Harrell estate. The 21st Return, filed by Fanny Harrell in 1940, indicated a balance in the hands of her guardian of $12,995.57 and a balance in bonds of $11,745.57. Tragically, Susie Harrell was never able to benefit from the funds so carefully invested by her sister.

As fate would dictate, Susie Harrell outlived all of her brothers and sisters. Fanny passed away in 1968 at the age of 94 and Susie in 1969 at the age of 92. For 52 years of her life, Susie had been locked away from society in Milledgeville State Hospital. The nephew of Susie and Fanny, Charles E. Strickland, applied for Letters of Administration on October 4, 1971 to settle both estates. The 250-acre Harrell farm, owned one-sixth by Susie and five-sixths by Fanny, had been valued at $126,500 in 1968.

Susie Harrell was buried at Westview Cemetery in Atlanta in an unmarked grave in the plot of her parents, Newton and Mary Harrell. Her brothers Jasper and Charley, Charley's wife Julia, and sister Fanny also share the plot. And though her interment was unpretentious, one may hope that Susie Harrell's strong spirit rejoiced after being held captive to mental illness for over half a century.

The next individual fits the category of "inspired" and invites one to marvel at his ingenuity. He could also be classified as a pioneer. Definitions of that term may encompass the concept of this writer, who believes that a pioneer—regardless

William Penn Patterson designed the first school buses for Chestatee School. Pictured at center, Patterson adapted a truck body to serve transportation needs.

of the time in which he or she lives—will adapt his occupation, indeed his entire lifestyle, to meet the needs brought about by the changes of his day. William Penn Patterson was just such a person; by every right, he could be labeled a true pioneer.

What was William Penn Patterson's family background and during what era did he reside in Forsyth County? In 1845, Patterson's great-grandfather married Darcus Cockburn in Forsyth County, thus establishing a long line of descent that extended down to the 1930s. The following was written by Penn Patterson's grandson Ted Paxton before he was elected sheriff of Forsyth County in 2000:

> My grandfather, William Penn Patterson, is pictured standing in front of his bus. He is the one in the middle. As I understand it from my mother, he was the leader in stepping forward and organizing the building of the first school buses for Chestatee School.
>
> In addition to being the local blacksmith, he also owned a store. They lived on the Cumming–Gainesville highway near where Harmony Grove Church is now located. The homeplace, store, and blacksmith shop were all together. The store and blacksmith shop were near the road, with the house farther back.
>
> My grandfather's parents also lived on the same property. My grandfather was born there August 16, 1893. The entire family lived in the area. He married my grandmother, Gertrude Bennett, who was also from Forsyth County. They had three children: my mother, Virginia

Patterson Paxton; daughter, Evelyn Patterson Kinsey; and son, Heyward Patterson. My mother and father live in Tucker; Evelyn lives in Forest Park on the south side of Atlanta; and Heyward resides in Gainesville.

My grandfather, Penn Patterson, was a very ingenious person with strong community ties. My mother said from her earliest recollection she remembers they always had electricity, even though the EMC had not gotten electricity into the rural areas. My grandfather had a generator which produced electricity for their house and the other family homes on the property.

The store he operated, in addition to the blacksmith shop, was basically a grocery store. He did carry a limited supply of dry goods, such as cloth. The store was a trading center for area residents. Many times he would be in the blacksmith shop or out driving the school bus when customers would come by the store. There was a bell out front which they would ring and my grandmother would go down from the house and wait on them.

The school buses were built with the help of the other gentlemen pictured. My grandfather, being the blacksmith, basically designed the buses as they went along. They had no formal plans to build from. The bus which he personally drove was built from a Dodge truck body which he bought from the Nalley dealership.

In 1938, he sold his portion of the property and moved the family to Flowery Branch in Hall County. His parents remained at the homeplace. The reason for their moving is as follows. My grandfather entered into a business agreement with Mr. Worth Connor of Flowery Branch. Mr. Connor had a large tract of land which he wanted to clear. My grandfather agreed to build and operate a sawmill in Flowery Branch to achieve this venture. Every day for approximately six months he would leave home and drive to Flowery Branch to operate the sawmill. Eventually, he realized this venture was going to take three to four years to complete. He had no desire to make that journey everyday so he convinced my grandmother the sensible thing to do would be to move to Flowery Branch.

She was reluctant but finally agreed when faced with the incentive of more modern conveniences. Even though he [William Penn Patterson] had a generator which produced electricity, it was only enough to run the lights. They could not have a refrigerator or other appliances. Flowery Branch had electricity and therefore they would have full power. My mother remembers him promising my grandmother an electric iron. Up until then she had to rely on an iron which she heated on the hearth. He drove to Atlanta just after the move and purchased the iron for her . . .

My grandfather was an outstanding person who stood on his principles, always stepping forward to help out in the community

without expectation of reward or recognition. I am honored to have
known and learned from him.

Even though he moved his family to Flowery Branch, he always
kept Forsyth County as his home. He would constantly drive back to
Cumming to trade and buy goods. Dr. Mashburn was his doctor and
he would never go to any other doctor. . . . When he fell ill in 1977,
he made my mother take him back to Cumming to Dr. Mashburn. He
spent several weeks in the hospital here until he passed away, just before
his 84th birthday.

The next story could be entitled "Forsyth County Had No Railroad . . . but
Trains Wrecked Lives."

It's true. Forsyth County doesn't have a railroad, but there were two near
misses. Don Shadburn in his Pioneer History of Forsyth County, Georgia
related that, in 1853 and 1854, the idea was conceived to extend a rail line from
Atlanta through Cumming to Dahlonega and perhaps, eventually, to Rabun
Gap. A corporation was formed to sell stock in the Forsyth and Lumpkin Rail
Road Company, but, alas, the necessary capital was never raised and the efforts
to establish the line were put on hold until after the Civil War. In the 1870s and
1880s, the dream resurfaced, but to no avail. To this day, Forsyth Countians
must look to Buford–Gainesville on the east and Ball Ground on the west to find
railroad tracks and depots for freight or passenger service.

One should not be deluded, however, into believing that citizens of Forsyth
County and their extended families have escaped the tragedies so frequently
associated with railways. Whenever reports of an Amtrak disaster flash across the
television screen, the viewer may be reminded that trains have also wreaked havoc
in the lives of Forsyth Countians from Civil War times to the modern day.

Not all railroad disasters have arrived in the form of train wrecks and loss of life.
For example, Ansel Strickland, son of pioneer settler and successful gold miner
Henry Strickland—who migrated to the Forsyth County area with brothers Hardy,
Oliver, and Talbot, and sister Nancy Harrell—endured numerous difficulties as a
child as a result of the Augusta Railroad. Born in May 1858, Ansel was orphaned
at the age of five. His sister Laura and her husband John B. Richards attempted
to keep the family together. A few years after the Civil War, Captain Richards,
guardian of Ansel and his brothers, invested the boys' part of their father's estate
in railroad stock of Augusta, Georgia. When this investment failed, all of the boys'
money was lost. Though Ansel matured into a fine physician and prominent
citizen of Cumming, he nevertheless struggled for years to obtain his education
and elevate himself to the status he later achieved.

When railroad history is recalled, the infamy of the Brockett Road crossing in
Tucker will ever be present in the minds and hearts of the Bailey family, who
lost seven members in one train-car tragedy. On February 17, 1964, Samuel
Monroe Bailey, age 41, his wife Pauline Missouri Bailey, age 37, and five of
their children—Brenda Ann, age 16, Betty Ann, age 8, Wanda Gail, age 6, Cathy

Ann, age 5, and Thomas Wayne, age 3—were killed as a train crashed into the automobile in which they were riding. The couple's three remaining offspring, Samuel Monroe Bailey Jr., age 18, David, age 12, and Jerry, age 11, were not with the family at the time of the accident.

As friends and family looked on in shock, a row of seven caskets, which varied from adult to child-size, awaited burial in Concord Baptist Church cemetery in the Silver City community of Forsyth County. Today, the tombstones of these crash victims are grim reminders that an automobile is no match for a moving locomotive.

A few years after the Baileys of Stone Mountain were struck and killed at Tucker, another train-car accident occurred closer to home. On November 8, 1970, the lives of five students from Forsyth County High School were snuffed out at the Highway 20 crossing in Buford when the car in which they were riding was struck by a Southern Railway passenger train traveling from Washington to Atlanta. At an extremely dangerous location, the crossing had been the site of 10 deaths in the 15 years prior to the tragedy. As Forsyth County mourned the loss of its young people, the *Atlanta Constitution* voiced its concern in the following editorial:

> The fact that this tragedy occurred at a railroad crossing near Buford which has had accidents before will prompt many to ask whether it

Caskets were lined up in Concord Baptist Church cemetery as family and friends awaited the burial of members of the Bailey family killed in a train wreck at Tucker.

might have been prevented. The crossing has stop signs but no flashing signals, no bell. Gwinnett County officials more than a year ago called it one of the most dangerous in the area and suggested that this crossing and others might have to be closed.

But nothing was done. And the price was five young lives.

Something was later done. A concrete bridge now spans the railroad, but not before Peggy Sue Daniel, age 16, Patricia Gail Holtzclaw, age 15, Linda Lou Holtzclaw, age 17, and Kristie Martin, age 15, were buried in Sawnee View Memorial Gardens. Cathy Sue Holtzclaw, age 14, was laid to rest in Oak Grove Baptist Church cemetery. Perhaps, after all, Forsyth County did not need rail lines to cause further grief to the families of hapless victims.

On a more upbeat note, the following focuses on an impulse. Occasionally—just once in a great while—a fleeting thought will occur to someone, and, after due consideration, that individual may deem his idea to be an inspiration worthy of follow-up. Such was the case when Dr. Rupert Bramblett and his patient (and relative) Clarence Holbrook were engaged in conversation while Bramblett was visiting at the Holbrook home one evening in 1959.

Dr. Bramblett per chance mentioned that the new president of the American Medical Association (AMA), Dr. Louis Orr, was a physician from Florida. To

Dr. Rupert Bramblett had been visiting Clarence Holbrook when he had the inspiration to invite the president of the American Medical Association to a meeting at Cumming. Holbrook is pictured with his daughters Lonieze and Gertrude.

Bramblett's utter surprise, Clarence Holbrook, who had previously resided in Florida for a number of years, declared that he knew Orr well and had been his patient for an extended period of time. Then, Holbrook added that Orr had been born in Cumming in the house owned and occupied, in later years, by the Bryan Redd family. (Orr had related this to Holbrook when he learned that Holbrook grew up near Cumming in Forsyth County.)

The renowned Florida urologist was on Bramblett's mind as he drove home that evening. Before reaching his destination, he was struck with the idea of inviting Orr to address a meeting of the Chattahoochee Medical Society, a group of less than 25 physicians from Gwinnett and Forsyth Counties, at a location near Orr's birthplace.

Bramblett, as secretary of the medical society, sent the invitation the following day. Almost by return mail, Bramblett received a letter of acceptance from Orr. Then, AMA headquarters went into extensive action, with its staff initiating numerous phone calls until definite plans could be finalized in a time-frame satisfactory to the schedule of AMA. Numerous secretaries and assistants to the president of the AMA also required consideration. Bramblett remembers that some of the individuals who called him sounded somewhat less than wildly enthusiastic about the AMA president meeting with a small number of people in a little town in Georgia. Everyone was polite, however, in a businesslike manner.

Transportation was arranged from Atlanta, to the meeting site, and back to Atlanta. Orr entered his native Cumming in style, for Dr. and Mrs. Marcus Mashburn Sr. met Dr. and Mrs. Orr in Dr. Mashburn's nearly-new Cadillac sedan and, subsequent to the meeting, returned the distinguished couple to the Ansley Hotel in Atlanta.

The Chattahoochee Medical Society meeting was held in the Forsyth County High School building, only a few blocks from the Bryan Redd House on Kelly Mill Road where Orr was born in 1900. The guest of honor, introduced to the gathering by Dr. Marcus Mashburn, later commented that this was the finest introduction he had ever received. In addition, he made the heartfelt remark that, of all the speeches he had delivered to audiences—both medical and political—as president of the AMA, this one was somehow different and meant more to him in some peculiar way than all of the others.

9. MEDICINE

From the early days of the county to the present, Forsyth has been blessed with dedicated physicians and the quality of patient care that these individuals could render as determined by the medical advancements of their day. Several families of doctors—including the Lipscombs, Mashburns, Hockenhulls, and Brambletts—have served their communities for decades, while numerous other physicians have devoted their lives to the well-being of others.

In the town of Cumming, Dr. Ansel Strickland, a far-sighted physician whose career spanned the late nineteenth and early twentieth centuries, established a practice based on scientific precepts. Before exploring Strickland's application of these principles for the advancement of science, one would do well to examine the background of this unique Forsyth Countian. From whence did he come and what experiences may have shaped his progressive ideas?

Born in May 1858, Ansel Strickland was the son of Henry and Elizabeth Smith Strickland. One of the most successful miners in North Georgia, Henry Strickland had married Elizabeth Smith, a native of Massachusetts and daughter of Daniel Smith, one of the first merchants of Cumming. Ansel, born in Cherokee County, Georgia, was their youngest offspring.

Strickland may have come from distinguished ancestry, but, nevertheless, his boyhood was far from ideal. Orphaned at the age of five, he was reared in Cherokee County, where he received his primary education before enrolling in a school in Norcross. Strickland's medical education was gleaned through reading medicine and attending lectures at Atlanta Medical College from which he graduated in 1881. Strickland then relocated to Cumming, Georgia, where he established an enviable reputation for skill based on unusual success.

On the subject of smallpox, Strickland was adamant in his belief that the disease could be wiped out.

> The Germans have proven that smallpox can be eradicated from a nation. How? Simply by vaccination. By vaccinating whom? By vaccinating those who have not had smallpox. When? Before they become infected with the smallpox germ. Whoever heard of a doctor being so silly as to try to vaccinate a man after he had contracted smallpox in order to

prevent him from having the smallpox, for as the table is round, you cannot round it.

Preventive treatment, to Strickland, was the only viable solution for halting the spread of infectious diseases such as rabies.

> Now there are two, or rather three, preventative treatments. The first . . . was the one adopted by Germany, to wit: Have all dogs muzzled. That is a good treatment. The second . . . is compulsive vaccination of all citizens over five months old with herbivorous hydrophobia virus, which would make all men immune. Third: make compulsive vaccination of all dogs with herbivorous hydrophobia virus, thereby making all dogs immune.

Strickland was particularly zealous in attacking scientific problems, such as the depleted soil in farming areas. Writing analogously, Strickland admonished farmers in the use of fertilizers:

> The trouble in the fertilizing question is simply a misunderstanding on the part of the farmer, as to what a commercial fertilizer is. Commercial fertilizers are made up of chemicals and, so to speak, simply stimulants.

Dr. Ansel Strickland was a prominent physician of Cumming. He applied scientific principles to the practice of medicine.

Dr. Jim Bramblett, son of Martin T. Bramblett, practiced medicine at Crabapple and later in Oklahoma.

> To make it plain, common corn is a food to man's body, but ferment it, then distill it, and you have it in the form of a stimulant only, no food whatever. Then you have it this way: Guano is to land what whiskey is to man; manure is to land what corn is to man.

Strickland was not always so serious, however. Even he needed a respite from the burdens of the day and the low points in his life. In 1907, he bought the second automobile in the county and thoroughly enjoyed it for several years prior to his death. The auto, manufactured by International Harvester Company, is now in a museum in Jonesboro.

Not only had Strickland experienced tragedy during his boyhood, but misfortune overtook him during early adulthood as well. In 1879, he married Julia Hockenhull, daughter of Dr. John Hockenhull. The couple soon suffered the loss of three children, and then their daughter Charlotte was born in 1888. But in 1889, Julia passed away and was laid to rest in Cumming Cemetery with the three lost infants. Strickland chose as his second wife Mamie L. Rogers, daughter of Captain R.N. Rogers of Milton County, Georgia. Married in 1891, the Stricklands were blessed with five offspring: Roy E., born in 1894; Ellene, born in 1897; John, born in 1899; Clifford, born in 1905; and Lynn, born in 1908. Strickland passed away on January 7, 1914.

From town to the country, a call from the yard or a knock at the door, someone in the immediate community or several miles away was in need of medical assistance. And what was the response? In the era of the country doctor, a home visit was required. To be more specific, in the days of Dr. Martin Truman Bramblett, the physician would seize his medical bag and hitch his team—or relegate the job to one of his sons—and depart for the home of the ailing individual. And if per chance the hour was late, he would mount his lantern on the buggy behind his two mares, Mag and Meg, to light the way over rough, dusty roads or through ruts deep in mud and mire.

Martin Truman Bramblett, born on April 28, 1853, married Indiana Hawkins, the daughter of Robert Hawkins, on April 1, 1874. Approximately 11 years later, he graduated from Atlanta Medical College and began the practice of medicine. His office, which was used primarily for storing medicine, was located across the road from his home on what is now Dr. Bramblett Road (so named for his son Dr. Rader Hugh Bramblett).

Dr. Martin Truman and Indiana Hawkins Bramblett had nine children, three of whom became doctors: Emma Lenora "Nora" Bramblett, Dr. James C. Bramblett, Truman Alexander Bramblett, Artie Mae Bramblett, Dr. Rader Hugh Bramblett, Dr. Joel Thaddeus Bramblett, William Corbett Bramblett, Nettie E. Bramblett, and Samuel D. Bramblett, who died in infancy.

The second child of Martin and Indiana Bramblett, Dr. James C. Bramblett, was born on March 19, 1877. He married Sarah Eugenia Vaughan on December 25, 1900 and the couple raised nine children. According to Jim Bramblett's youngest daughter Virginia, her father worked his way through medical school by driving a streetcar in Atlanta and working in a marble quarry during the summers. He and his wife also took in boarders to provide for his medical education.

James Bramblett graduated from Atlanta Medical College—the forerunner of Emory University—in 1908 and practiced for a time at Crabapple. From there, he moved to Meansville, where he and his wife divorced. Subsequently, he went from Atlanta to Kansas and finally to Pocasett, Oklahoma, where he resided and practiced medicine until his death in 1945.

Dr. Joel Thaddeus "Thad" Bramblett, another son of Martin Bramblett, was born on August 3, 1889. Having graduated from the college of Eclectic Medicine and Surgery in 1911, Thad Bramblett practiced for a time at Coal Mountain and at Matt in Forsyth County before he migrated to Oklahoma. On September 30, 1909, he married Naomi Sams. They were the parents of two children. On October 25, 1924, Thad Bramblett died tragically in an automobile accident in Oklahoma.

The year 1911 marked beginnings and endings for the Brambletts. Both Joel Thaddeus Bramblett and his brother, Rader Hugh Bramblett, graduated from the Georgia College of Eclectic Medicine and Surgery and launched their careers in the medical field. Their father and mother both passed away during the same year. Dr. Rader Hugh Bramblett, the third physician son of Martin Bramblett, was born on October 5, 1886; he married Ida Palestine Garrett, daughter of John

Alvin Garrett, on December 18, 1904. Rader Bramblett and his wife resided on what would later (after his life had ended) be named Bramblett Road, where the couple raised their two children. Having graduated from the Georgia College of Eclectic Medicine and Surgery in 1911, Rader Bramblett entered into a lifetime career of practicing medicine in Forsyth County.

On to the next generation. The son of Dr. Rader Hugh and Ida Palestine Garrett, Rupert Harold Bramblett, was born on September 6, 1918. He graduated from the Medical College of Georgia in September 1944; served as Grand Master of the Georgia Masons in 1966; served on the Forsyth County Board of Education from 1949 to 1952; was a member of the Board of Directors and a member of the House of Delegates of the Medical Association of Georgia; received the Medical Association of Georgia's Distinguished Service Award in May 1998; and is currently serving on the Advisory Committee for the Franklin D. Roosevelt Little White House at Warm Springs, Georgia.

On June 1, 1998, Rupert Bramblett retired from the practice of medicine after serving the citizens of Forsyth County for 53 years, thus ending 113 consecutive years of Bramblett physicians in Forsyth County. That same year, Rupert Bramblett described the life and times of the country doctor:

> I am Dr. Rupert Harold Bramblett, a fifth generation resident and third generation physician of Forsyth County, Georgia. Those who live in our thriving, rapidly growing, prosperous county cannot imagine what it was like when I was a child—or for that matter, as late as the mid-20th century. Although my father was a busy physician, practically all of his patients were farmers. In fact, there was nothing else to do in Forsyth County except farm. There was no industry. Nothing else existed here, and, except for the storekeepers—and some of them farmed on the side—payment for anything one did depended upon the farmers. Furthermore, the area was not well-suited for farming, and poverty was widespread. It was even widely accepted.
>
> There was only one native of the community where I grew up who finished high school when I was a child. She [Hannah Holbrook] immediately started teaching in grammar school in a one-room schoolhouse and was my teacher for a few years—actually the best teacher I ever had. In later years, she was my patient until she died a few years ago.
>
> My father and the other doctors in those days did very little office practice. Most of the patients were treated in their homes. The dirt roads—and there were no other kind—were rough when dry and in many areas absolutely impassable when it rained. Wooden bridges were carelessly built across the creeks with no elevation of the roadway on either side of the stream and when much rainfall came, the creeks would flood the roads, often times making them totally impassable. On a larger scale, the same thing happened to the rivers.

Dr. Rupert H. Bramblett, third generation physician, is the son of Rader Hugh Bramblett and the grandson of Martin T. Bramblett. On February 14, 1978, he married Annette Schroeder, the author of this volume.

During the winter in the early 1920s, my father's Model T Ford car was in need of repairs and someone had carried him to a home several miles away to an obstetrical patient. As sometimes happened, the patient was in slow labor and he was there all day and all night before completing the delivery. Mother and baby were fine and the man was carrying my dad home. It had rained hard and had turned very cold, and when they came to Settendown Creek one mile from our home, water was across the road on both sides of the bridge and the man would not drive his car into it, afraid that the water would drown the engine, as they used to say, and they would be stranded in the water.

My dad was worried because he knew that there was little firewood at our house when he left, expecting to be back home in several hours, and his fears were well-founded. My mother, at home with two children, this one very small, used up all the available firewood, and when she asked her brother-in-law who lived next door to cut some wood for her, he told her it was too cold to get out and cut firewood, to move into their house. This she thought she could not do. The local telephone lines all converged at our home, and she was afraid to leave them unattended. Someone needing to know where to find the doctor would be calling there.

Well, it was a bad situation. When the man would not drive into the freezing water, my dad removed his shoes and socks and waded through it, breaking the skim of ice on top as he waded into the water, and the skim of ice on top as he waded out on the other side. The weather was so cold that after he put his socks and shoes on and started up the road, he could hardly walk. By the time he climbed the hill and ran into the first house where a neighbor lived about a half a mile from our house, he knelt by the open fire and cried as his almost frozen feet began to very painfully regain circulation.

When he reached home, my mother told him that she was sorry but she had found it absolutely necessary to burn some old furniture—an old wooden bedstead from the back room to keep a little warmth in the house. My dad said, 'That's all right, honey. If it ever happens again, you can pull the siding off of the house and burn the weatherboarding. Just be careful to start first on the side away from the wind, and maybe I'll get home before you get around the corner." My dad's fee for that delivery was $5.00, and of course he may not have ever been paid anything.

Even by the time I started the practice of medicine in Forsyth County in 1945, there was only one paved road in the county—Highway 9, going from Atlanta through Cumming and on to Dahlonega. Although we did have some improved, so-called gravel roads, many were not and even the gravel roads broke down when prolonged winter rains occurred. I made house calls almost daily, starting in the early afternoon

Dr. Rader Hugh Bramblett, son of Martin T. Bramblett, resided at the Bramblett home place in Forsyth County and conducted most of his practice through house calls. Pictured with him is his wife, the former Ida Palestine Garrett.

after a full morning's work in the office and it was often far into the night—sometimes after midnight—before I returned home. It was not unusual to visit the sick in 20 or 25 homes, located in two or even three counties, and, in bad weather, I might have to find someone with a team of mules—rarely a tractor—to pull my car out of mud holes two or three times in one day and night.

An interesting event occurred after my dad was older and the roads were better and he worked in his office until noon, as I did when I started my practice in the county, then ate lunch and started visiting patients' homes. This was in 1943 while I was still in medical school, my father was called on an emergency just as he was about to leave on his round of house calls. Two young men, one of them AWOL from the Marines, had fatally wounded and robbed a storekeeper [Ben Roper] about three miles from our home, and while Dad was working with the patient before sending him to the hospital in Atlanta, two young men came to my parents home and asked Mother to see my father. She told them he wasn't there—he had gone on an emergency call. Well, they waited around in the yard near his office until my dad returned, and he just paused briefly to see if there were any added calls that he had to make before going on the round that he had already promised. One of the men told Dad that he needed to get medicine for his sick baby. Ordinarily my father would have opened his office and gotten the medicine for him, but fortunately he felt compelled to get started on his previously promised home visits. Delayed because of the emergency call he had made, he probably told the young man to come back later that afternoon and then rushed off to visit sick people in their homes. It was learned later that the two young men were the very same two who had robbed and fatally wounded the storekeeper, and their victim died a few days later in an Atlanta hospital. After they were captured, one of them told the authorities that their plan had been to get my father into his office, overpower or kill him, and use his car for their getaway.

Well, my granddaddy, my daddy, and I all were doctors in this county, starting in the spring of 1885. . . . And we were all dedicated to service for the people who trusted us, always doing our best for them, whether they paid us or not in the days before Medicare and Medicaid, insurance payers, HMOs and the whole conglomeration. Along with other doctors of the time, we were privileged to know that we were held in high esteem.

During the era prior to the mid–twentieth century, the physicians' motto might well have been "have medical bag, will travel," but physicians treating patients in the homes would soon be a thing of the past.

In the 1940s, Forsyth County could boast a private hospital when Dr. Marcus Mashburn Sr. converted the Mashburn Hotel into a health care facility. After he began delivering babies and treating patients in Mary Alice Hospital, as the institution was known, his two sons Dr. Marcus Mashburn Jr. and Dr. Jim Mashburn joined him in caring for patients when they had completed their residency training at Grady Hospital in Atlanta.

But even greater health care changes were in store. Following the passage of the Hill-Burton Act by the United States Congress, the Forsyth County Hospital was erected through public funding in 1957 with Dr. Rupert Bramblett serving as its first chief of staff. The facility on Samaritan Drive remained a county-owned and operated hospital, offering a wide range of medical services, until it was sold by the county commissioners in the 1980s. Subsequently, the institution passed through for-profit owners and experienced a name change to Lakeside Community Hospital. Then, in December 1992, Georgia Baptist Hospital purchased and renovated the hospital. Thereafter, it was known as Baptist North.

When Georgia Baptist took charge of the hospital in Forsyth County, improvement in health care became readily apparent. Not only did Baptist North, as the facility was renamed, strive to provide quality care and service to area residents, but it became actively involved in the community as well.

To offer Forsyth County even more services, Baptist North—under the leadership of Administrator John Herron—undertook the arduous task of obtaining a Certificate of Need (CON) from the state to construct a new state-of-the-art facility. Numerous hurdles in the form of appeals from area hospitals having been cleared by December 28, 1996, the health care group received its letter of approval at the end of January 1997, permitting it to proceed with plans for a new building.

The grand opening for the 41-bed hospital on Highway 20 near the Georgia 400 exit, originally estimated to cost $18.6 million, was held on March 12, 1999. Luckily, the structure was erected with expansion in mind, for with the growing population and increased demand for medical care in Forsyth County, Baptist North would need to grow as well. And grow it has. The Georgia Department of Community Health approved a CON for an additional 37 beds in May 2001 at the renamed Baptist Medical Center. As objections from area hospitals were dealt with and put aside, plans materialized for renovating the third floor and adding a fourth at an approximate cost of over $11 million. Then came further developments when Georgia Baptist announced that the hospital would be sold. To whom, at what cost, and under what conditions? The hospital saga in Forsyth County continues to unfold.

An interesting side note, Dr. W.R. Dunn is the only physician from the early years of the Forsyth County Hospital to serve on the staff of Baptist Medical Center and the only one of that group to remain in practice today. Dunn rejoined the Mashburns at their clinic when the Forsyth County Hospital had been open just a few years, after a period of service as a missionary in the Belgian Congo.

10. African-American History

The events of September 1912 shaped race relations between African Americans and whites in Forsyth County for decades, even into modern times. But before one delves into the multiplicity of misdeeds which occurred during 1912, that individual should first become cognizant of the times and examine the events in the context of the period.

History records that, in 1906, a race riot had resulted in terror and mayhem in Atlanta. Then, a few years later, Gainesville was beset by racial unrest. It is little wonder then that the citizens of Forsyth County, being somewhat uneasy, would react strongly to the egregious deeds of certain African Americans.

The trouble began, as newspapers reported on September 7, after two African Americans purportedly criminally assaulted a white woman 5 miles outside of town in the Big Creek district. *The Atlanta Journal* related that "the young white woman, who was living with her mother, after retiring Thursday night was awakened by the presence of a Negro man in her bed. Her screams frightened the Negro away and he and his confederate fled."

The two perpetrators, along with four other African Americans, had been hunted down, apprehended, and placed in jail without incident. Then, an African-American preacher, Grant Smith, began to cast aspersions on the character of the victim, an act that enraged the citizens of the area. Smith was "horsewhipped" almost to death by an angry crowd. Shortly thereafter, he was placed in the courthouse vault for his own safety. African Americans attending a barbecue in Cumming retaliated by threatening to dynamite the town. The situation might have deteriorated further had troops from Gainesville and Marietta not rushed to the scene. Martial law was declared in Cumming and quiet was temporarily restored to the community. It was later reported that Toney Howell, one of six prisoners who had been taken from the Cumming jail to Marietta for security reasons, confessed to the crime and was scheduled for trial at the February term of court.

"Temporarily restored" as applied to normal tranquillity is an apt description, for, on September 9, the report of another assault on a white woman—this one so vicious that a skull fracture resulted in her death—appeared in print. The rape and murder of Mae Crow in the Oscarville community occurred less than one week after the assault on the young woman at Big Creek.

The rock in the forks of the tree is purportedly the one used to inflict fatal wounds to Mae Crow.

On Sunday, prior to the *Gainesville News* report of September 9, at about 12 p.m., Earnest Knox, alias Daniel, assaulted Mae Crow while she was on her way to her aunt's home to assist her mother in returning to her home with children. Having dragged the young woman into the woods, beaten her over the head with a rock, and raped her, Knox left the unconscious Crow and went to meet with friends on their way home from a Sunday afternoon church service. Around midnight, two other African-American men and a woman, who carried a torch to light the way, sought to find Crow's body. Still barely alive, Crow was raped a second time by the two men.

The following morning, Crow was discovered about 9 a.m. in a pool of blood. Dr. John Hockenhull and Dr. J.P. Brice were immediately summoned, but alas, too late. Mae Crow succumbed to her injuries that same afternoon. Meanwhile, Ernest Knox confessed to the dastardly deed and was rushed to jail in Atlanta for his own safety.

On September 11, the *Gainesville News* described the scene in Cumming. An angry mob of several hundred men, who had gathered at the jail, stormed the structure and shot one of the prisoners, Ed Collins [*sic*] and mutilated his body with a crowbar, whereupon he was dragged through the town and hanged with a rope around his neck to a telephone pole diagonally across from the courthouse. Collins, it must be noted, had been charged with accompanying Knox to the body of Mae Crow for the purpose of disposing of the remains in the river. The body of the African-American male, which had been left hanging on the telephone pole, was removed by county officials and taken inside the courthouse for an autopsy. The hanging victim would later be identified in the *Atlanta Constitution* as Bob Edwards. According to historian Donna Parrish, Edwards is also the name given on the autopsy report.

Two hours after the lynching of Edwards in Cumming, the mob started to Marietta where six African Americans were being held, including Ernest Knox, who had been taken there for safekeeping. The five arrested in the Big Creek incident—Fate Chester, Tony Howell, Isaiah Pirkle, Joe Rogers, and Johnny Bates—were removed from the Marietta jail to the Fulton Tower in Atlanta in anticipation of violence after a phone call from Cumming apprised officials in Marietta of the situation in Cumming. Apparently, the mob learned of the removal of the prisoners, for the rush to Marietta ended before its destination was reached.

A short time later, a trial followed for two of the perpetrators of the attack on Mae Crow. Those who had been arrested included Ernest Knox, two other African-American men, Ed Collins, and Delia Daniel, the mother of Ernest Knox, who purportedly held the light used during the second rape of Crow. On September 30, Oscar Daniel was indicted for rape and Ernest Knox for rape and murder. The trial that ensued was like none that Forsyth County had ever witnessed, for it was conducted with a military guard around the courthouse, three companies of the Fifth Regiment patrolling the square and searching all who entered the confines of the courthouse fence.

As the trial proceeded, the evidence presented against Knox was a small mirror purchased at Shackelford's Store, which was found near the dying woman. Unexpected testimony, however, from the sister of Oscar Daniel clinched the verdict for both defendants. It was the same woman, Jane Daniel, whose common law husband Bob Edwards had been lynched following the assault. Without advising counsel, Jane Daniel proceeded to give an eye-witness account of the second rape with sufficient details to convict the two on trial. And the sentence? On October 4, Superior Court Judge N.A. Morris pronounced that, on October 24, 1912, the two should have a private hanging for their heinous crimes. Hang they did, but private it wasn't. A fence had been erected around the gallows on the property of Dr. Ansel Strickland, but a group of white individuals, acting on the desire of the citizens of the county to witness the execution, burned the fence and allowed full view to all who assembled on the hillsides for the hanging. Families gathered from throughout the county, quietly witnessed the execution, and peacefully and calmly departed to their homes thereafter.

Then an assault of a different nature took place. The Atlanta newspapers severely criticized the hanging—sans fence—and tended to berate the citizens who were on hand to witness the event, to which an irate Dr. Strickland replied:

> The daily papers of Atlanta are hunting for something sensational
> to print, regardless of the truth or who it hurts. These papers have

> slandered the entire population of this county and sent it out to the reading world. They have cast a stigma upon you and your children that will go down to the fourth generation. . . . The editor of the *Constitution* could not have done you nor your women near the harm if he had spit in their faces.

The aftermath of the trial was equally as dramatic, indeed farther reaching, than the trial itself. Written notices having been placed in mailboxes, on trees, and thrown on doorsteps, post-haste African Americans could be seen exiting the county with their belongings until almost all of them were located elsewhere. The question then arises as to how their property—real estate—was settled. Decades-old rumors to the contrary, each and every parcel of land was sold, with the proceeds going to the African-American owners. All of these individuals may not have received "fair market value" for their property, but deed records in the Forsyth County courthouse indicate that the land was sold and deeds recorded in a legal manner.

That racial mistrust persisted for years is an understatement. However, on August 14, 1924, the *Forsyth County News* printed a letter to the *Constitution* from J.E. Puett of Cumming:

> I beg to advise that I have talked with city and county officials, and also with quite a number of citizens of different parts of the county, and the opinion is almost unanimous that it is entirely safe for tourists with Negro chauffeurs to pass through Cumming and Forsyth County with no fear of being harmed or intimidated. . . . The good people of Cumming and Forsyth County regret exceedingly the impression that has gone out regarding our present attitude towards the colored people.

Before the subject of the exodus of African Americans from Forsyth County is put to rest, it must be made abundantly clear that there were numerous white citizens who wished this group of people to remain because some of them were descendants of their former slaves and because of the valuable contributions some of these individuals offered to their respective communities. Charlie N. Harrell, the grandson of pioneer Edward Harrell, even went so far as to mention the injustices done to some of the African Americans in an explanation of items in his will of June 29, 1950:

> I believe the darkies that were run out of Forsyth County, Georgia, about 1912, were as law abiding citizens as lived in any county in Georgia at that time. Some owned their homes, some had rented, some had started plowing and preparing for planting; most all had some plans for the year. Very few, if any, had any place to go; some had never been out of the county. Some of their homes and churches were burned, some of the graves of their dead, left behind, were mutilated. Nothing done about

Would-be spectators lined up outside the courthouse fence to await their turn to be searched. No one was allowed to enter the courthouse grounds with a weapon.

it; apparently, no law against it. If there had been such a law, one that would have ensured every law-abiding citizen in the U.S.A. against loss of life or property at the hands of any illegal mob, there would have been no such mob. At least, that is what I think about it.

I am old and lived there. All along I have had the feeling that these darkies should at least be paid back the expense and loss they were put to, in having to leave their homes and jobs, because a Negro, said to be from South Carolina, brutally murdered a white girl in that county. Nothing could have been worse. But the Forsyth County Negroes had no more to do with it than you or I. Yet they were forced to take a loss that has never been repaid. And, so far as I know, their loss was written in the skies, in the winds and hearts of thousands of human beings; also in the heart and mind of Uncle Sam. Who knows? I don't, but this I do know: It is why it is written in my will.

What little, if any, that I may leave them, would not be a drop in the bucket toward paying their losses. It is only a gesture, to say I have always had a friendly, sympathetic feeling for them and every other law-abiding citizen who had suffered their fate.

Fast-forwarding 75 years, from 1912 to 1987, Forsyth County once again became a staging ground for groups wishing to gain publicity for their messages. The Brotherhood Marches, as they were called, drew the attention of not only the state and nation, but the world to events which had occurred in Forsyth County decades before.

The January 17 march with Hosea Williams, well-known Civil Rights leader of Atlanta, and 75 black and white marchers who were unfavorably met by members of the Ku Klux Klan, was but a prelude to the production that was to follow one week later.

With television cameras rolling and the world focused on the town of Cumming, Williams returned on January 24 to lead a march of 20,000 Civil Rights demonstrators from a local shopping center to the town square, where speeches emanated from the steps of the Forsyth County courthouse. Anti–Civil Rights groups of every sort converged on the town from neighboring states and beyond. On hand to ensure the safety of all groups were 1,700 National Guardsmen, ordered out by Governor Joe Frank Harris, 148 State Patrolmen, 150 GBI agents, and 300 troopers stationed around the square, not to mention local lawmen under the direction of Sheriff Wesley Walraven. For the most part, citizens of Cumming and Forsyth County stayed at home.

And what was the outcome of the marches? A Bi-Racial Committee was established, which prepared an extensive report concerning events that had impacted African Americans since the turmoil of 1912. Census records and property records were examined. A valiant attempt to end animosity between the two races was undertaken. Meanwhile, on the heels of the march, Oprah Winfrey kept the eyes of the world on Forsyth County by taping her show from a local restaurant and prolonging the emotional climate precipitated by the marches.

The Brotherhood Marches were not the only visits to Forsyth County by African Americans, for individuals and families came to examine courthouse records, to search for cemeteries, and to glimpse first hand the area where their ancestors once lived. One such family included the descendants of Jim Strickland, who once resided in the Shakerag/Sheltonville community and was a valued citizen of southeastern Forsyth County, and his sister Loucinder Strickland, who married a Cohen. Jim and Loucinder Strickland were the offspring of Lucy Strickland and an overseer—a Davidson or Macy—on the Strickland Plantation.

On August 1, 1998, Strickland descendants held a rededication ceremony at the graves of their ancestors to affect closure to the events of 1912. Twenty-eight members of the family gathered for prayer and to light candles and lay flowers on the unmarked, but clearly visible, graves located on property on Old Atlanta Road now owned by the Nichols family (purchased from the Buices in 1949). The land on which this ceremony took place had been purchased by Ezra Buice from the Findley family years before. Interestingly, even with the property transfers and tension between the races, which existed in the first half of the twentieth century, members of the Strickland family had years later returned to Forsyth County to bury their dead. This time, they had returned to honor the memory of their ancestors.

11. TWENTIETH CENTURY AND BEYOND

The Fowler farm in south Forsyth County typifies the changes that have occurred in land usage over the past century. When Alonzo Fowler began acquiring land in 1909, he, as well as other farmers in the area, raised a large family that cultivated a vast acreage in cotton crops.

In 1922, Fowler erected a stately one-and-a-half-story, nine-room, temple-front cottage on his property and outbuildings concomitant with the rural lifestyle. Subsequent to Alonzo Fowler's death in 1934, the land passed from his wife to his youngest child Glenn, who already resided there with his wife, the former Helen Benson.

Changes were just on the horizon for agriculture in North Georgia, and the Fowler farm would be a part of those changes. Cotton, which was never suited to North Georgia anyway, would soon become impractical as a cash crop with the land depleted and prices on the world market at rock bottom. What was a farmer to do? Glenn Fowler made the essential adjustments when he switched to "growing" chickens, planted fescue in the fields, fertilized the fescue with litter from the chicken houses, and raised cattle on the lush pastures produced by this system. The Fowler farm was proof that the new "crops" could increase the standard of living for the rural families from the late 1930s and beyond.

To follow the history of the Fowler property further, Glenn Fowler passed away in 1999 and the 277-acre tract was later sold to the Forsyth County government for a site to construct a sewage treatment plant and park, and to preserve the dwelling house and outbuildings—smoke house, garage, barn, corn crib/cow shed, chicken houses, and tenant house—as examples of a way of life from the now bygone agricultural era.

Recognizing the need to preserve a farmstead in the county, the Historical Society of Forsyth County nominated the 10 acres containing the house and outbuildings to the National Register of Historic Places. At this writing, the nomination has passed the State National Register Review Board and is included on the State Register. In a few months, the reformatted nomination is expected to reach Washington, where it will be considered for listing on the National Register.

Meanwhile, the house is not sitting untended, for Forsyth County Public Facilities Director Frank Halstead is supervising the rehabilitation of the structure. In Halstead's capable hands, the dry wall added in the 1950s has been removed to expose the original tongue and groove boards, the electricity has been upgraded, and heating and air-conditioning are being installed. Contractors are soon to replace termite-damaged wood and substitute old materials in place of the modern baseboards and molding, which were a product of the 1950s. When the rehabilitation is complete, the Forsyth County Parks Department plans to occupy the dwelling; in addition, the historical society will set up displays to enable visitors to learn about the Fowlers and farm life in years past.

The Fowler House is not the only historic structure Frank Halstead supervises. The bandstand on the courthouse square is also maintained under his watchful eye. Loved by the citizens of the county for decades, the Cumming Bandstand, built in 1915 with private funds as a location from which the Cumming Brass Band could perform concerts, is the oldest structure on the square. It was erected by carpenter John Robbs and used for Sunday afternoon performances until the band members departed the county to serve in the military during World War I. Later given to the city of Cumming, the bandstand converted to county ownership after seven years because it stands on county property. Regardless of

The Fowler House was built in 1922 by Alonzo Fowler for his wife, the former Mittie Lena Blackstock, and children. His youngest son Glenn and wife Helen Benson Fowler continued to reside in the structure until their deaths.

ownership, the charming structure has served as the site for political speeches, weddings, fescue festivals, and musical performances by school groups—to name only a few uses over the decades—and has been restored and maintained by the county government, the Cumming Garden Club, the historical society, and now the Public Facilities Department of the county government. The bandstand has been nominated to the National Register of Historic Places and, like the Fowler property, has passed the Georgia National Register Review Board and will soon be reviewed at the national level.

If one associates the bandstand with musical performances, that individual doubtless remembers the June Singings in the old 1905 courthouse. In preparation for the events, which were held annually on the last Sunday in June, singing groups practiced diligently. Equal attention was given to the outfits to be worn, the singing being *the* dress-up occasion of the year in Cumming. As the day arrived, so did folks from far and wide. Parking was at a premium with the overflow from the square extending all the way to the Baptist Church. An apt description of the day in 1924 included the following tidbits from the *Forsyth County News*: "Tom, Dick and Harry, Mary Rose and Henrietta; were all on hand from Buford, Duluth, and Alpharetta. . . . A number of people never hesitated to say; that the Singing was like a big homecoming day."

Still focusing on downtown Cumming, the appearance of the town square was dictated in part by deterioration, in part by fire, and, at times, by some businesses giving way to others. The Farmers and Merchants Bank, which operated from prior to the end of the nineteenth century to well into the twentieth century, was advertised for sale in 1923:

> A certain lot located on the National Highway in the Town of Cumming, Georgia, and fronting 45 feet on the north side of said highway, and extending back north of uniform width a distance of 72 feet. This tract has a two story brick building located thereon and is known as the bank building and the Henry Hurt storehouse.

"Cumming Ablaze" is an apt description of the fate of the town structures from time to time. Arson was blamed in the 1920 fire that destroyed the store building of George Heard and the homes of Ezra Johnson and J.P. Bannister. In 1924, the cause was deemed an accident when an oil stove in the store of Bagley and Poole exploded, consuming not only the store building, but the Mashburn Hotel, W.E. Lipscomb's office, Mollie Kemp's millinery shop, the Bank of Cumming, and the telephone exchange. Then, in 1934, a fire that had been discovered in the store building of R.P. and I.C. Otwell destroyed that building, plus the S.M. Stripland Drugstore and Claud Brooks's Grocery.

Scarcely a decade has passed since the fire of 1934 that Cumming has not reported losses from burning buildings. From the Ivan Otwell house in the 1940s to the Georgia Power fire around 1950 to the city hall fire, which destroyed city records, and numerous others, including Parson's Store in 1982, fire damage and rebuilding have been an integral part of the history of the town. But the courthouse fire of 1973 was perhaps the one blaze that most affected the citizens of Forsyth County, necessitating the erection of the present courthouse, which was completed in 1978, and creating a sense of loss that would continue for many years.

Fires aside, another area that required development and expansion county-wide was road building. From pig trails to gravel roads, impassable in inclement weather, the need arose for paved highways as the population became more mobile. Until 1933, no paved road existed within the borders of Forsyth County and the dirt roads that spidered their way across the county were worked either by the citizens themselves or prisoners in the chain gang. In May 1930, a group of citizens—Judge R.L. Bagley, Postmaster A.C. Kennemore, Warden George J. Barrett, and Cumming Mayor Roy P. Otwell—trekked to Atlanta to implore the aid of state highway officials. The delegation visiting Governor Eugene Talmadge and J.J. Mangum of the State Highway Board were assured that Highway 9 between Atlanta and Neel's Gap would soon become a reality. Then, with the completion of the north-south route in the mid 1930s, attention focused on establishing a paved east-west highway from Cumming to Canton. This feat having been accomplished in the 1940s, other county roads were paved slowly but surely, until virtually no unpaved roads existed into the twenty-first century.

Electricity, another modern necessity, came to Forsyth County in stages. Some homes in rural Forsyth boasted a Delco system. To serve Cumming, in 1923, a dam was constructed at the Kelley Mill place and work began on the installation of an electric lighting plant for the town. Then, in August 1929, Cumming was all "lit up" when Georgia Power turned on the current brought in from its lines in Buford. The rural areas of the county followed in 1938 as Forsyth County Electric Membership Corporation, later known as Sawnee EMC, threw the switch to bring electricity to 451 homes on 168 miles of line at an approximate cost of $125,000.

During the same period, the Soil Conservation Service was beginning experimentation with crops such as kudzu, to help hold the soil along roadways and assist farmers to build dams to enhance their farmland. Incidentally, the success of kudzu gave way to the more practical planting of Kentucky 31 fescue, which thrived on the depleted soil of roadways and pastureland, especially when fertilized with chicken litter.

Success and chickens went hand in hand near mid–century. Dr. Ansel Strickland is credited with growing the first "hot house" chickens in the county. In the early days, with farmers accustomed only to yard chickens, a number of methods were tried. One that proved highly impractical was the construction of the two-story chicken house, one of which still exists on the Fowler farm today, though not in use.

Mayor Roy Otwell was instrumental in convincing Wilson and Company to locate in Cumming, thus establishing a nearby poultry processing plant for the convenience of local farmers and a boost to the county's economy as well.

Who were the pioneers of the poultry industry? Names such as J.C. Vaughn, Reverend Frank Vaughan, Lester Sexton, Eldo Grogan, George Bagley, Arthur C. Smith, A.C. Smith Jr., Clyde Pendley, Jeff Heard, Mark Heard Sr., Mark Heard Jr., Ben Wofford, H.R. Bramblett, George W. Pirkle, Paris Bennett, George Bramblett, Ralph Otwell, Roy Otwell, D.O. Freeman, Clay Freeman, George Welch, Jay Holbrook, Henry Stripland, Joe Martin, Leland Bagwell, Dean Ledbetter, Hubert and Clay Cowart, Roy Holbrook, Ralph and Paul Holbrook, Inmon Smith, Reverend William Flanagan, Reverend Charlie Gazaway, Reverend Ford Phillips, and R.C. Vaughn come to mind. Operating early hatcheries were the Corn family, Glenn Cox, and Ben Wofford.

From an agricultural background sprang the Forsyth County Fair. In 1950, the fair, sponsored by the Cumming Kiwanis Club with Agricultural Agencies cooperating, was located "between the cannery and the pole barn." By modern day landmarks, the fair would have been on the parking lot in front of the Detention Center and up to the backs of the county buildings on East Maple Street and over to the fire station on Veterans Memorial Boulevard. Just what did the event offer fair goers? In addition to the competition in food preservation and handiwork, there was to be an exhibit from the Farm Group, the Mad Cody Fleming Shows and fireworks to "rock the town with a beautiful display."

From fun to serious changes, the county in 1957 witnessed two significant events that impacted the area for decades to come—dedications of the Forsyth

Alonzo Pendley stands in front of one of the oldest chicken houses in the county. The building, with a capacity of 500 chickens, was owned by Joe Nix.

County Hospital on August 17 and Buford Dam in October. As county residents of today examine conditions of 50 years ago, they are incredulous that no hospital existed in Forsyth County until the Mashburn doctors opened their private facility, Mary Alice Hospital, in the mid–1940s. During the subsequent decade, with the growing needs of the county and advances in medicine, a county-owned hospital became increasingly essential. Dr. Rupert Bramblett and Dr. Marcus Mashburn Sr. took the initiative and spent countless hours of their own time canvassing the county for votes for the bond election, which would provide the county's portion of funds to erect a Hill-Burton hospital.

Under the nationally legislated Hill-Burton Act, the federal government would pay one-third, the state one-third, and the county would be responsible for the remaining third of the funding for the medical facility. At that time, Forsyth County was not the affluent area that it has become. Citizens were reluctant to commit to a bond issue. But, fortunately, bonds received an affirmative nod from voters in December 1955, and construction began on the 32-bed hospital, which was estimated to cost $450,000, but which was actually built for approximately $410,000. The dedication was held on August 17, 1957 with Hon. Phil Campbell, Commissioner of Agriculture, delivering the keynote address. The *Forsyth County News* described the "bragging points" of the hospital thusly:

> The building is completely air-conditioned and has a stainless steel kitchen which can be used for an expanded facility when and if needed without any additions. It has a spacious lounge and lobby with the best

The power house at Buford Dam, dedicated in 1957, generates electric power from its reservoir known as Lake Sidney Lanier.

furnishings available for the comfort of those who have members of their family or friends here. Complete x-ray facilities are available in the new hospital in a separate room.

The medical staff of 1957 was composed of five doctors and two honorary members. Dr. Rupert Bramblett served as the first chief of staff. To further quote the local newspaper: "As the new hospital opens, it has a complete staff to take care of patients who are admitted and all the facilities and comforts of the best hospital anywhere."

Side by side with the newspaper announcement of the opening of the county-owned hospital came a second announcement—that of the dedication ceremonies to be held in October for Buford Dam, a reality after years of political maneuvering at the federal and state levels. Property had been purchased from private citizens, the dam had been constructed, and Forsyth Countians had observed the flooding of Lake Sidney Lanier.

On August 22, 1957, plans for the dedication were revealed. Ceremonies were scheduled for October 9, with Georgia's Senator Richard Russell as the principal speaker. Other dignitaries for the occasion would be Senator Herman Talmadge, Governor Marvin Griffin, and Representatives Phil Landrum and James C. Davis. In addition, public and civic leaders connected to the Buford Dam Project and its promotion and development, and leaders from other nearby counties, were expected.

Placing the October 9 event in historical perspective, the *Forsyth County News* provided this synopsis of the project as it had progressed:

> Built by the Army Corps of Engineers, Buford is the northernmost dam and the control structure in the Chattahoochee-Appalachicola-Flint River system. Work on the dam has been under the district engineer of the Corps of Engineers at Mobile, Alabama. Ground was broken in 1950. The final construction project, the powerhouse, is ready to operate.

With the opening of the hospital and the dedication of Buford Dam, the citizens of the county were in a mood for celebrating. On July 4, 1958, a local steam engine owner decided to hop aboard his engine and drive around the square in Cumming. An idea was born. Cecil Merritt is credited with promoting the first real parade when, on July 4, 1962, A.G. Thomas, Roy Thomas, and Gene Bennett drove their engines around the square with five boys on bicycles following. Merritt, who had built radio station WSNE in 1961, set up a radio loop in the bandstand and broadcast the parade from that vantage point. Merritt continued to manage the parade until he retired. The Mashburn-Thomas Steam Engine Parade, as it is known today, is an event unique to the region. Huge crowds lining the parade route each year have attested to its popularity through the years—with old and young alike enjoying the celebration.

In 1973, the parade made its way around the square without a courthouse in the background, for arsonists had destroyed the brick structure that had served the populace since its dedication in 1905. It would be five years and several bond elections later when voters approved a bond referendum for $1,590,000 and a new courthouse could be completed on the site.

The story of the 1905 courthouse is not quite finished, however. Before the old courthouse was built, plans had called for a grandiose three-story structure to grace the town square. But, as frequently occurs, funds were short and the plans, of necessity, were scaled back. However, the magnificent building is now under construction. Under the leadership of long-time Cumming mayor Ford Gravitt, all eyes are on the north block of the square as a new building is taking form—to be the new Cumming City Hall. And how does this building appear? It resembles both the 1905 courthouse and the one originally proposed. A dream has become reality almost 100 years later.

July 1, 1998 marked another milestone for Forsyth County, this one involving its judicial system. Previous to that date, Forsyth had been included in the Blue Ridge Judicial Circuit. However, with a burgeoning population and a burdensome case load, relief was needed in the courts. Hence, the Bell-Forsyth Judicial Circuit was created and named in honor of one of the county's most distinguished citizens, Colonel Hiram Parks Bell—author, statesman, soldier, and Mason.

Forsyth County was fortunate that the new circuit was created in 1998, for a population explosion has seized the county and created pressing needs in its wake. In recent years, the story has been one of the area garnering the dubious distinction of "fastest growing" since the turn of the twenty-first century. One may credit a number of factors: Lake Lanier attracting those seeking recreation; Georgia Highway 400, constructed in the 1970s, luring a segment of the working people who commute to Atlanta on a daily basis; scenic beauty; excellent schools; and the list goes on. Likewise, both the city and county governments are working arduously to keep pace with growth. Indeed, Forsyth County has made the transition from rural to suburban, its population now a staggering 100,000.

BIBLIOGRAPHY

BOOKS AND ARTICLES

Bagley, Garland C. *History of Forsyth County, Georgia, 1832–1932. Volume I.* Easley: Southern Historical Press, 1985.

———. *History of Forsyth County, Georgia, 1832–1932. Volume II.* United States: Boyd Publishing Company, 1990.

Baker, Carolyn Nuckolls. *A Brief History of Brown's Bridge.* Unpublished manuscript prepared for the Historical Society of Forsyth County, 1999.

Bottoms, Roy. "History of the Franklin Gold Mine." North West Georgia Historical and Genealogical Society. Volume 5, Number 4 (October 1973): 3-7.

Chappell, J. Harris. *Stories of the States: Georgia History Stories.* Atlanta: Silver Burdett and Company, 1905.

Colliers, Mrs. Bryan Wells. *Biographies of Representative Women of the South. Volume 3.* Self-published, 1925.

Coughlin, Robert David. *Lake Sidney Lanier: A Storybook Site.* Chelsea: BookCrafters, 1998.

Croy, Eugene. *Pine Top Fox.* Cumming: Self-published, 1976.

Kester, Vaughn. *The Prodigal Judge.* Indianapolis: Bobbs-Merrill, 1809.

Malone, Henry T. *Cherokees of the Old South.* Athens: The University of Georgia Press, 1956.

McConnell, Reatha Sosebee. *Friendship is Reaching Out.* Cumming: Self-published, 1990.

Shadburn, Don L. *Pioneer History of Forsyth County, Georgia.* Roswell: W.H. Wolfe Associates, 1981.

Tallant, Winnie. *Migration of Holbrooks from England to America and Forsyth County.* Cumming: Self-published, undated.

Wade, Forest C. *Cry of the Eagle.* Buford: Moreno Press, Inc., 1969.

White, George. *Statistics of the State of Georgia.* Savannah: Publisher unknown, 1849.

DIRECTORIES AND MISCELLANEOUS

Articles in the *North Georgia Star.* 1996–2001.

Georgia General Assembly, 1880–1881. *Biographical Sketches.* Published by the state of Georgia.

Georgia State Gazeteer. 1883–1884.

Historical society's loose papers in the *Garland Bagley Collection.*

King, Francis P. *Gold Deposits of Georgia.* Unpublished report, 1896.

Manley, Kate et al. Unpublished Kelly manuscript.

Moravian Diary entries. February, 1809. Diaries by Moravian missionaries.

Sheltonville-Shakerag Records Committee. *History of Sheltonville.* Self-published, 1962.

Tatum, James Roosevelt. *Tatum.* Unpublished manuscript, 1959.

Transcript of trial of Josiah Phillips. Records of the state of Georgia, county of Forsyth, 1941.

Transcript of trial of Austin Watson and Walter Fowler. Records of the state of Georgia, county of Forsyth, 1943.

Yeats, W.S. *Gold Deposits of Georgia.* Unpublished report, 1894.

NEWSPAPERS

Atlanta Constitution, 1912–1964.

Atlanta Journal, 1912.

Baptist Leader, 1892.

Forsyth County News, 1911–1957.

Gainesville Herald, 1884.

Gainesville Times, 1969.

New York Times, 1991.

INDEX

A new Cumming City Hall is under construction——built to resemble a courthouse that was proposed in 1904, but never constructed due to insufficient funds in the county's coffers.